The Spoken Christ

The Spoken Christ

Reading and Preaching the Transforming Word

Willard Francis Jabusch

CROSSROAD • NEW YORK

1990

The Crossroad Publishing Company
370 Lexington Avenue, New York, NY 10017

© 1990 by Willard Francis Jabusch

Printed in the United States of America

Library of Congress Cataloging-in-Publication Data

Jabusch, Willard
    The spoken Christ : reading and preaching the transforming word /
Willard Francis Jabusch.
      p.   cm.
   ISBN 0-8245-1015-1
   1. Preaching. 2. Word of God (Theology) 3. Bible—Reading.
4. Lay readers. I. Title.
BV4211.2.J285   1990
251—dc20   90-31112
                                          CIP

"There is one God who manifested Himself through Jesus Christ His Son, who is His Word, proceeding from silence."
—St. Ignatius of Antioch
Letter to the Magnesians 8.2

CONTENTS

PREFACE

An elderly woman stands in a gallery of the Louvre and gazes intently at the great masterpiece of the late Middle Ages, the *Pietà* of Avignon. She neither knows nor really cares about the "information" concerning the painting, that it was painted for a Carthusian monastery chapel in the south of France or that art historians think they may know at last the name of the artist. Also she gains little new "information" from the painting itself. It is, after all, a familiar subject in Christian art. Who has not seen numerous reproductions of Michelangelo's version in books and churches?

Why then is this great Gothic painting so important for this woman who contemplates it with such devotion? It does not inform her so much as it transforms her. Through the power of its color, composition, and dramatic line, the tragic scene is made real and present for her. She is "in communion" with Jesus and Mary; she becomes aware at a more profound level of what she already knew: that Jesus suffered a cruel death to save us, that Mary's heart was pierced with grief at the loss of her innocent son.

It is not especially important who painted this mighty picture so long ago, since it achieves what so many inferior and uninspired works fail to do. It not only communicates a religious message or stirs up pious emotions, but it also brings us into communion with Jesus and his mother.

The old woman seems close to tears. She is obviously deeply moved. Does she think of a child killed in an accident or in the war? Perhaps she realizes that the grief of Mary is shared today by everyone who must witness the suffering of the innocent. Does she feel not only the sorrow of Mary and her own pain and resignation, but also the painful death of the brothers and sisters of Jesus who are killed by poverty, plague, death squads, ignorance, and indifference?

The *Pietà* does more than communicate the facts of Calvary. It brings the viewer into communion with the Lord and his people. It does more than inform us about how Mary held her son at the foot of the cross. It transforms us, changing the way we see our lives and the rest of the world.

If this is the aim of the greatest Christian painting and sculpture, it is also the ultimate aim of the spoken word in Christianity. The oral reading of scripture and the preaching in Catholic, Protestant, and Orthodox churches clearly would do more than instruct us. (An atheist may, after all, be brilliantly informed about the life of Christ and the Bible.) The "spoken Christ" in Christian proclamation comes to transform us and live in us. We are brought into a deep communion with the Lord.

Of course the word can do many things. It is rich and powerful and not to be chained. It can instruct and persuade, bring hardened hearts to conversion, and inform us of Christian dogma and morality. In fact, during this time of great ignorance concerning basic Christian beliefs, teaching the ignorant is not the least of its functions. But for the Christian, the spoken word can do still more.

Early Christian writers felt there was something sacramental about the proclamation of the word of God. Caesarius of Arles in the early sixth century put it this way:

> I ask you, brothers and sisters, tell me which seems the greater — the body of Christ or the word of Christ? If you wish to answer accurately, you must say this: the word of God is not less than the body of Christ. Therefore, as the solicitude which we observe when the body of Christ is ministered to us is such that not a particle of it falls from our hands to the earth, so, too, with as much care should we see to it that the word of God, which is His gift to us, does not perish from our heart, while we're thinking or talking about something else. Because we will be no less guilty.[1]

Like the sacraments, the oral interpretation of the scriptures and the preaching which follows it bring us into contact with Jesus Christ.

Even in this world of computers, space ships, and nuclear dangers, the "spoken Christ" wills to come in order that we may have life and have it more abundantly. He is not content to have his word enshrined in Hebrew or Greek. He would speak in the idioms of those today who sit in the shadow of death.

Death, of course, can take many forms: personal and institutional sins, routine and indifference, drugs and violence, ignorance and bigotry. Father Gustavo Gutiérrez has helped us see that poverty itself equals death: physical death from lack of health care, mental death from lack of education, cultural death from a lack of leisure and beauty, moral and religious death from a lack of pastoral care and opportunities for worship and contemplation.

Clearly, bringing the "spoken Christ" and his abundant life into a world of death and darkness demands a speaker who dares to go beneath the surface of the text to be interpreted, who looks at the world with courage and honesty, who knows that "no one gives what he or she does not have," and who has a sense of the holiness and dignity of this task.

And so this is not a "how-to-do-it" book. There are already many fine texts on the techniques of oral interpretation, public speaking, and preaching. Rather it is an investigation of the opportunities and the obstacles, the challenges and the necessary qualifications for our brothers and sisters who are chosen to serve the "spoken Christ" today.

By the very fact of baptism, all Christians are called into the service of the "spoken Christ" by preaching the gospel to all the world, giving the Lord his "voice" as a new millennium arrives. But some accept special responsibilities. Readers or "lectors" stand up in the Christian assembly to interpret prophets and epistles, cantors sing out the psalms and hymns, and the clergy enter the pulpit to preach. It is to all of these that the following pages are directed, to Catholics and Protestants, men and women who share the task of bringing words of abundant life to those who are in danger of dying.

Yes, men and women! It is probable that the majority of lectors in many churches are already women; however, it is also true that the number of women who preach regularly is still very small. Our pronouns may be, therefore, more or less inclusive. It seems certain, nevertheless, that even in those churches where the ordination of women still seems somewhat remote, their gifts for preaching will be used more and more in the years ahead. For the "spoken Christ" does not demand that his message be heard only in the tenor, baritone, or bass registers!

If the *Pietà* of Avignon, a wondrous etching by Rembrandt, or a magnificent icon by Rublev can draw us into the presence of God, opening our hearts to a glimpse of the divine beauty and compassion, then surely our proclamation of the word of God should do no less. In this we are, according to Paul, "coworkers of God!"

· 1 ·

A QUESTION OF COMMITMENT

The house lights dimmed in the majestic old Auditorium in Chicago. The theater Frank Lloyd Wright said has "the best acoustics in the world, bar none" was filled to capacity. It was to be an evening of lieder performed by Dietrich Fischer-Dieskau, the celebrated German baritone. He walked to the piano and began to sing the Schubert song cycle, "Die Winterreise."

Something very astonishing happened. The singer created a world of beauty and wonder, of sorrow and longing, of the pain of love and of life. And we, the audience, willingly entered in. In twenty-four songs, we were taken on a strange and moving journey, through many shifting emotions, through subtle changes of mood. The singer's power was hypnotic and almost frightening as he sang the final song, "Der Leiermann." All those hundreds of people, the majority of whom probably knew no German, felt nonetheless those piercingly poignant and stark closing lines:

> Wunderlicher Alter,
> Soll ich mit dir gehn?
> Willst zu meinen Liedern
> Deine Leier drehn?
>
> Strange old organ grinder,
> Shall I come with you?
> Will you play your organ
> When I sing my songs?

1

It was a concert such as many dream of. It was not merely a "willing suspension of disbelief" in the story of romantic love and grief. Rather, a communion had been achieved between singer and listeners and text. Of course the music and the poetry were themselves important (although the texts by Wilhelm Müller are not extraordinary), and of course the splendid singing voice of Fischer-Dieskau was a delight. But these were not the deciding factors in this experience of empathy and communion. Other fine vocalists have done these same songs without attaining equally profound results. If we should not "tell the dancer from the dance," that night we could not tell the singer from the song.

If it were not merely vocal technique or richness of tone, then what made this man's interpretation so special? What made the difference? It can be, I think, summed up in this: commitment to the text.

The singer had entered deeply into the text, discovering its meaning, its moods, its changes, no matter how subtle and shifting, and had convinced himself of the importance of these words and the emotions they convey. He had found in himself the same or analogous feelings and experiences. He had come to believe in these lines which he would sing and had become committed to them. Although always with great precision and control, he was willing to identify with the restless and melancholic "persona" of the poems.

Although, quite frankly, the sensibility portrayed in "Winterreise" is hardly that of many people today, through the skill and, above all, the commitment of Fischer-Dieskau to these texts empathy and communion were made possible.

If a secular performer, working with some unexceptional lyrics of love and longing, can show such dedication to his craft and achieve such a deep response to his material, can the lector in the Christian assembly be less committed?

Does it happen in your church on Sunday morning? Does the miracle of "empathy" take place? Do those hundreds of people in the pews start to feel the same feelings and think the same thoughts as the ancient authors of the biblical text and the contemporary man or woman who orally interprets it? Do they share in the fire of Stephen and Paul as they preach, in the ecstasy of the Old Testament poets, in the agony and joy of the psalms? For surely deep human realities and the wonders of God are revealed in this most powerful of literature. But are they experienced by the congregation?

It is true that the lector is not an actor. But he or she is an oral interpreter of literature of great importance. Lectors must not superimpose something novel on top of the text, but they must certainly interpret fully the richness that is waiting in the text. Oral interpretation of the strong, biting, beautiful, visionary words of the Old and New Testament is not a job for a timid child of any age.

The lector has accepted certain responsibilities in the Christian community. It is never a trifling thing to stand up before a large number of people, demanding that they give their time and attention to an oral interpretation of a written word. To interpret orally any text, sacred or secular, means a serious attempt to give to an audience the full intellectual and emotional content of the passage. However, if the reader of worldly literature does not make this attempt or, having made it, does not succeed, the results are usually not grave. An audience is, perhaps, left unenlightened or not entertained; a certain amount of information is not given or an experience of beauty is not shared. But the consequences are usually not tragic. Yet, for a Christian community, cursed with lectors who either do not know their responsibilities or cannot fulfill them, the results are dire indeed. The nourishment that should come from the word of God is not received. A kind of spiritual malnutrition sets in. An ennui and disdain for the Bible follows; the words of scripture produce only a boring tastelessness. The whole liturgy begins to appear as a formality, heavy and unreal. Can it be saved by good preaching or fine singing? Perhaps. But the subtle message has been given that we need not really care about the word of God and its communication. It seems an unhappy waste of time, a burdensome job to be endured. The views of those who think of "liturgy as pain" or even "religion as mockery" are again reinforced.

If poor reading in church were merely a waste of time for five hundred or a thousand parishioners, it could more easily be tolerated. However, it is hard to be tolerant of the incompetent (though almost always "well-meaning") lector when he or she is seen as a noxious and stifling influence on Christian life, paralyzing the minds and hearts of the faithful, killing their spirit and their gusto for both the Bible and the Lord who speaks in its varied books.

Let us picture the familiar scene. A reader, neatly dressed, of no little education and poise, walks to the lectern before the large Sunday congregation. We may also suppose that he or she is not suffering from any voice or diction problems, that bodily movements are not bizarre, and that the microphone is turned on and functioning well. The congregation is quietly seated, waiting in hope. But let us ask the lector a simple question at this point: "Just what do you intend to do in the next few moments?"

He or she answers politely, "I am about to read a passage from the Bible."

"But, my friend, why precisely do you want to do this?"

There is a pause.

"Well,... the pastor asked me to do it... and besides, we always have a reading at this point!"

It would seem that a reading is done for the same reason that a hymn is often sung or a sermon preached — it is customary. And the result is the customary, totally expected numbness of the listeners. Nothing really happens, only the sounding of words on the airwaves. There is no change or movement in the heart, no increase of understanding, no excitement of the spirit, only a further atrophy of devotion and religion. Of course, it is not quite true to say that this Sunday's readings have made no difference whatsoever — they have indeed contributed to an unconscious sense of frustration and withering of faith!

The lector must clearly know what he or she would achieve. What is the real purpose of this weekly effort of reading aloud ancient texts to an assembled people?

We read aloud in order to interpret as richly and fully as possible what the author wanted to say. We want a particular audience to experience the full meaning of a text from the Bible.

The full meaning of a text? What the author wanted to say? Does the lector really know what the author (in this case, a very ancient author) wanted to say? Do the words of Amos and Isaiah, Peter and Paul, Luke and Mark and all the others truly mean something to the reader? Does he or she understand their vocabulary? Feel the force of their arguments and their rhetorical tricks? Clearly grasp their allusions and illustrations? Respond to their poetry as well as their faith? Is he or she acquainted with their theological assumptions and "world-view" — the way they see God and man and life?

Can the lector feel the emotions that impelled those people of long ago to speak in the first place, the deep and shifting feelings that support their words and which are as important as the logical meaning? A dictionary definition of words may be essential as a step to enter into the meaning of a text, but woe to the reader who does not go beyond this first step. To be given only theological ideas, only the concepts of Paul in his Letter to the Galatians, and nothing of his anger and his irony, the bite of his wit, is to be given a truncated text, an abused, abbreviated text, an ultimately unfaithful and therefore somewhat heretical text in which the word brings not life but death.

For in the Bible, as in all great literature, it is fundamentally impossible to skim off the ideas, to divide the matter from the means, to give, for example, a "theology of Paul" which is somehow "purified" from the passion and pain and ecstasy of the author. The oral reader who attempts to stay clear of the fury of Jeremiah ends up by not giving us Jeremiah. To avoid the shifts in feeling and to ignore the poetic devices of a psalm is to deny that the psalm is a song and poem — and therefore to negate both its importance and total meaning.

Much of the Bible is great literature and therefore it is a sensitive and accurate record of human experience. In fact, in a work so vast almost all of human experience is recorded: situations both gentle and violent, feelings both subtle and powerful, petty nagging and visionary shouts, terrible pain and the extremes of gladness. Since it is the record of Semitic peoples who habitually feel things deeply and intensely, and who are not at all shy about expressing their feelings, we can suppose that the more delicately shaded, the more sophisticated nuanced responses to a situation will be less featured than the bigger, dramatic, vigorous, and even violent reactions. Samson and Samuel, David and Bathsheba, Paul and John are, after all, not cool French intellectuals or Anglo-Saxon writers for the *New Yorker*. Anger and fury in the Bible are not presented in shades of fashionable gray. A bland TV news commentator will probably find himself choking on a juicy biblical curse! The vivid descriptions of Oriental life, of blood and battle, must not be read like a laundry list or a stock-market report!

But the readers hesitate, fearful and timid. How far should they go? Will they become a kind of actor? What about becoming overly emotional and melodramatic? Won't they be accused of turning the holy text into a cheap bit of theater and of personally "putting on a show"?

The only response can be — *go all the way in your effort to be faithful to the text!*

Of course, it is not the job of the lector to superimpose new ideas or new emotions on the biblical text. To do so would be a gross misuse of his or her position and an injustice to the people. But it is equally unjust to deny the people the full meaning of the text, the complete experience, the sharing in both the intellectual and emotional world of the author. The words to be spoken aloud in our Sunday liturgy are meant to inspire, challenge, instruct, delight, lead us to pity, to repentance, to thanksgiving and service, and to help us experience the wonders of God, bringing us to prayer and love. But none of this will happen without an emotional response to the text, first of all on the part of the reader and then on the part of the listeners.

When there is a deeply human response to the various cues in the text, when the voice and whole body (muscle response, facial expression, and gestures) are truly at the service of the sacred text, when the mind is alert and the heart is sensitive, when the reader is captivated by the text and knows its movement and color, when there is no longer fear about what "people will think" but rather a profound desire for communication and shared experience, then wonderful things start happening in the listening congregation. As people walk out of church toward the parking lot or the local pancake house, they remember a scriptural text that touched them deeply. And they are usually moved to comment not on the technique of the reader but rather on the power of the Bible which, to their surprise and delight, no longer seems tedious!

For if nothing else came out of the months and money that were spent back in the sixties on Vatican II, it seems clear that the Lectionary alone was worth it all! Before then, many knew almost nothing about vast sections of both the Old and New Testaments. Many pages of the prophets, most of the Gospels according to John and Mark, and so many other important scriptural passages were never read and never preached in many Catholic and Protestant churches.

Now, at least for those who go to church, there is the three-year cycle of readings that leads to a much more profound experience of the Bible. We are offered a truly generous sampling of both Old and New Testaments. But even more, we can now become involved in the story of our Father's saving love for his weak, yet wonderful, children. It is a story that begins long before Jesus but builds to a crescendo in his story and the record of his apostles' ministry. Little by little, we come to understand that this story is our story. And, rather suddenly, we hear the voices of characters in the story which surprise and challenge us. Frequently, in fact, what Jesus and the prophets say disturbs us and irritates our complacency.

Going to church on Sundays is no longer a soothing experience. We are forced to hear hard words from Jeremiah and Isaiah. Jesus tells about the inevitability of persecution and pain. His story of Lazarus and the rich man, for example, does not console us if we are among those who "feast every day." When these words are spoken in plain English they take on a force that they never had when chanted in the Latin of St. Jerome according to a stylized Gregorian formula. Even though we were allowed to repeat the gospel in English after singing it in Latin, there was an artificiality and a loss of strength in the repetition and, of course, many passages were never heard at all. A new clarity and urgency have come into the whole story of salvation. The inspired words about poverty, suffering, sinfulness, and liberation of the oppressed confront us again and again. But then so do the equally challenging words about forgiveness, the need for festival and joyfulness! There is little that comforts our melancholic mediocrity. There is nothing to support our selfishness and sadness.

Over just a few years the power of the story, especially that of Jesus, has been felt in much of the Christian community. Much superficial piety which could find no good foundation in that story has already become only a footnote in the long history of spirituality. Pretensions and pomposities that seemed normal when Jesus and the prophets were not clearly and regularly heard now appear ludicrous. Clergy and laity are forcefully judged by the very words that they speak in the liturgy. The sly

businessman or lawyer with dirty hands and heart finds himself
as lector reading Amos and Paul to the people! The self-satisfied
deacon, priest, or bishop discovers that he must read and preach
on words of Jesus that are clearly antiestablishment and quite
possibly anticlerical! It is not easy to insist on titles and trap-
pings after we are told to call no man "rabbi" or "father" or
"teacher." It is proclaimed, for example, that Jesus washed the
feet of his followers; the meaning is so clear that even a "pastoral
potentate" must feel the impact.

And what are we to do with the Lord's obvious predilec-
tion for the poor, his insistence on fidelity, and his teachings on
simplicity of life at a time when vows are facilely broken, our
style of life depends on galloping consumerism, and we back
governments notorious for their terrorism and exploitation in
the name of "good business" and expediency? If our self-image
is measured by conspicuous consumption much of the gospel
starts to stick in the throat.

This is no eighteenth- or nineteenth-century crisis of faith,
no intellectual wrestling match or moment of cool agnosticism.
When so much of the Bible was not read or preached it was possible to play scholarly games over isolated texts, to argue about
the credibility or authenticity of this verse or that. Now, on the
contrary, there is a cumulative and ultimately revolutionary effect. Now the substance of whole books are read, often in a more
or less continuous reading over a period of time. Old Testament
cuttings are balanced with gospel texts so that they reinforce
and complement each other. The thrust of the biblical message
is usually impossible to escape and, if we listen attentively and
try to respond honestly, it can cause a crisis. It is a vocational
crisis because it questions our fidelity to the Christian calling. It
is a crisis not of faith but of Christian living. It asks about our
identification with the great biblical story.

With whom do we identify as we experience this deeply moving and involving story? Do we stand with the "fat cats" of
Israel who were exposed and ridiculed by the prophets? With the
scribes and Pharisees who provoked Jesus to speak his harshest
words? With the urbane and immoral indifference of Pilate?

And if we identify with the prophets, the apostles, and Jesus
himself, can there be congruence between our models and our
morals? Or is the disparity too painful to endure, causing us

to leave our church, the place where the incongruities are so regularly revealed? If the church is no longer an atmospheric locale where duplicity is masked and sentimentality is nursed, it will not receive the warm attention or generous contributions of many people. In fact, like any other agent that causes grief and unrest, it will be viewed with growing disfavor and will be, at last, persecuted with vigor.

Unlike some believers in the thirties and forties who offered no widespread Christian resistance to Fascist evil, many Christians today have rather quickly been changed by the story of Jesus the Liberator which they hear again and again in the liturgy. The whole Bible is constantly forming them, making them sensitive to real problems and responsibilities. In Latin America, South Africa, and even in the United States of America, to preach and to follow the gospel have quickly become political and confrontational acts. Did the council Fathers in their reform of the liturgy realize that biblical proclamation and biblical preaching would, week after week, result in a transformation and an energy that was never possible in an earlier age of novena piety and "ferverino" preaching?

It can also lead, of course, to a martyr's death. The murder of Archbishop Oscar Romero while he celebrated Mass in his diocese of San Salvador is only one of many cases where the forces of darkness have furiously tried to extinguish the gospel light. The Bible and those who preach it are often considered subversive. Lay leaders who have preached good news to the poor and freedom to the captives have been marked for prison or death. It matters little if they be labeled "Communist" or "reactionary," "obscurantist" or merely a "nonproductive intellectual."

For the Christian story which is repeated again and again in ancient church or bamboo chapel always stands in the way of total power; it questions the given wisdom; it is a standing critique of any party line. It is not napalm or army flamethrower that must be feared by the forces of darkness and evil. Rather, it is the Liturgy of the Word which has at last begun to cast fire, chasing the shadows and burning the chaff. The fire that Jesus said he would enkindle on the earth starts to burn with a bright but uncomfortable flame. We open our Lectionary and the words rise and flash like dangerous sparks to ignite the world.

But after the Lectionary is closed, after the readings are over, what then? The reader has done his or her job. Now it is the moment for the preacher to step forward. What happens? A good place to find out is in the local pancake house where the folks gather for their Sunday "brunch," that new American institution.

"Our Pastor likes to tell stories. But to tell you the truth, they seem pointless most of the time."

"And if our priest preaches once more about his childhood and the wonderful family that he had, I may shoot him with a silver bullet."

"Do those priests realize the ten minutes they preach on Sunday are really the only time we will hear about religion? Why do they waste the opportunity by being 'cute' and inane?"

"Pastor X just retells the gospel story which, of course, he has just read. Does he think we are idiots?"

"Yes, but maybe that's better than the empty abstractions that we have to listen to every Sunday at our church."

"I think we senior citizens would be satisfied with a little spiritual help to get us through the week."

"But if you're in your twenties, like I am, and had only balloons and bubble gum in catechism classes and no real theology in high school or college, a little instruction in the faith wouldn't be out of place!"

"Instead of all that heavy 'bible stuff' I wish Father would use the sermon to explain just what the church does teach about marriage and weddings today. I know so much has changed!"

"Most of the clergy I know simply do not talk at all about what is right or wrong in family planning. Total silence certainly doesn't help those of us who still have some doubts on the subject."

"But I'd like to hear not just what the pope says about birth control but also what he says about social justice and the Third World. Why don't they preach about it?"

Why don't they preach about . . . ? Fill in the blank with your favorite subject: the charismatic renewal, abortion, nuclear war, liberation theology, the evils of the drug traffic, business ethics, or the rosary. In almost any parish these days, you will find a true rainbow of folks who sincerely wish that Father would courageously address what they consider to be important. From Catholics United for the Faith and Opus Dei members through those disenchanted with the Polish pope and those ready for a married female clergy, there is a plea for Sunday sermons that treat important (and often controversial) subjects.

But the clergy, on the other hand, are just getting used to giving "homilies." "We refuse," they protest, "to go back to the topical sermons that were the bane of pre-Vatican II preaching, a sermon on divorce, an instruction on 'mixed-marriages' or 'the commandments of the church,' a 'ferverino' on the apparitions at Lourdes or devotion to the Sacred Heart. We are now giving liturgical homilies rooted in sacred scripture and following the church year. If the people have a felt need for adult religious education or basic catechism lessons, let them be started in the evenings or Saturday afternoons. Don't try to put the blame or the burden on the Sunday homily. What happened to Christian books, pamphlets, radio programs, and discussion clubs? An inadequate C.C.D. or Sunday school system which has led to doctrinal and moral ignorance and confusion cannot be remedied by changing the homily back to an instructional sermon! The liturgy is not meant to be an information class!"

And so the debate steams on. Is it time to admit that while the homily is not intended to be a minitheology class, there is a need for substance? Although we should not return to the old three-year cycle of sermons based on the Creed, the sacraments, and the commandments, would it not be honest to admit that we are faced, in the average parish, with many people who know little of the belief of Christians, the purpose of the sacraments, and the challenge of Christian law and conscience? They are not hostile to religious teaching (or they would not be in the pews) but they are, for all purposes, untouched by it. The older folks often cling to what they learned as children, for they have heard only rumors of new approaches. The younger generation feels the pull of the Christian heritage but is quite ignorant of it. All sit in their places on Sunday with some hope of hearing a preacher speak to their needs. And one of their most urgent needs today is knowledge of Jesus, an understanding of his church, and an appreciation of the Christian heritage of prayer, ethics, and mission.

It's time to begin some serious "talking about Jesus."

• 2 •

TALKING ABOUT JESUS

The cars and trucks raced well over the speed limit. Did any of the drivers see the sign near the highway? It was a rather discreet sign, neatly lettered and not flashy. It simply stated "Jesus Is the Answer." Probably erected by some local Bible church, it sounded simplistic and trite, just a quaint relic of that American "old-time religion."

Perhaps. But is any Christian ready to say that the sign is false? Does anyone know of another valid answer to the questions that really matter in life? Amid the madness of terrorism and violence, hunger and despair, plague and nuclear disaster, is there really any other voice worth our attention? When faced with the realities of failure, sickness, poverty of incredible dimensions, a death of spirit and body, broken families and hopes, fears and heaviness of heart, do we as Christians know any answer other than Jesus and his way?

In fact, shouldn't everyone know the answer by this time? After all, the "Jesus" answer has been available for almost two thousand years. So many churches, so many pulpits, so many Bibles and books, and — most of all — so many millions of Christians. Why hasn't the news gotten around, at least in those parts of the world where there has been a strong Christian presence?

Those who have fallen away from Christian practice and those who have discovered Jesus "in the sects" suggest reasons. And strangely, their responses are similar.

"The fact is that we just didn't hear much talk about Jesus in the mainline churches. We heard talk about traditions and

innovations, about customs in the ancient Near East and ecclesiastical history, sociological statistics and psychological insights,
liturgical symbols and theological clarifications, and sometimes
even a little art, science, and politics. Stories were told and
myths were explored; there was a lot of theological reflection
and, more rarely, a touch of poetry. Some speakers were clever,
a few humorous, most were dull (a sin hard to pardon!); but the
fact is that we did not hear that much about Jesus so that we
might know him and love him."

"Faith comes through hearing," said Paul. Knowing and loving Jesus, trusting him and obediently following both his commands and suggestions, all that makes up "Christian faith" for
us, all this must follow an oral introduction, at least in most
cases. We must hear someone somewhere talking about him with
love and conviction. We must first become curious about this
man from Nazareth, then eager to hear more about him and the
good news he has for the poor and sinful. We must start to wonder at his call for unity and justice, for forgiveness and peace.
We must realize that he forgives us now, dwells with us now, and
at this very moment inspires us also to a life of unselfish love
and humble service. But we can do this only after we listen to
someone who has already experienced his presence and has at
least begun to respond to the gospel challenge.

In the normal course of things, there is no substitute for hearing "talk about Jesus" which is urgent yet kind, warm yet serene,
clear, strong, and heartfelt. It is this kind of talk, this kind of
preaching, that seems to be missing.

For far too many, sermons seemed to lead to death rather
than life. They stifled the spirit and led to confusion, depres-
sion, and guilt. Or merely to ennui. In fact, so many have been
deflated rather than animated by Christian worship (of which
the sermon is a part) that the mainline churches in the United
States lose sixteen thousand members every day!

But who is this Jesus about whom we must speak? Who is
this special and wonderful person we present as the "answer" to
the questions of our world?

Certainly there is only one Jesus, put to death after preaching and working in ancient Palestine, raised from the dead and
proclaimed as "Son of God" by his faithful disciples. But it is
also true that he has been perceived in different ways at differ-

ent times. In our talk about Jesus do we stress his humility or his grandeur, his humanity or divinity, his example of service or his eternal glory?

Is he the "Good Shepherd" as painted above the martyrs' tombs in the catacombs, beardless and youthful with the sheep who strayed held on his shoulders? Is he the great mosaic Christ high in the dome of a Byzantine church, stern of visage, his great eyes looking down to judge a sinful world and with imperial regalia as a clear sign of his majesty? Or is he rather the gaunt and tortured Christ of a medieval woodcarving, the "man of sorrows acquainted with infirmity," a victim of evil men whose repulsive and sadistic faces surround him as he carries his cross? Perhaps he could even be the classic Renaissance Christ, serene and in control even on the cross? Or Rubens's athletic Lord Jesus, full of energy as he conquers sin and death? Or are there still some who present the nineteenth-century "sweet Jesus" full of sentimental gentleness and void of anger and challenge?

American Protestants have long heard the preacher's cry to "take Jesus as your personal savior." Catholic preachers, of course, used a somewhat different vocabulary. But, after all, the "Jesus loves me, this I know 'cause the Bible tells me so" of Protestant Sunday school fame was not so terribly different from the "Good night, sweet Jesus" lyrics lovingly sung at the end of every Sorrowful Mother novena! The last two hundred years have been a time of spiritual individualism for almost all Christians. Jesus was offered in sermons, tracts, and hymns as the "answer" — but as a very personal answer for very personal problems.

In fact, in these later years we have had Jesus "the psychologist" present as the healing solution for middle- and upper middle-class neurosis. The Jesus for those who could afford "encounter groups" at Bethel or Lake Tahoe, freeing from "hangups" and bruised egos. The Jesus who blesses TV audiences from glass cathedrals and gets everyone "feeling good about themselves." The Jesus for "nice" people, i.e., comfortable capitalists.

But much has been changing. We are entering a new and very different period in the history of Christianity. It is a "third era" that confronts us with some radical new challenges — not least of all for preaching! We can say that the first period of the church's history and expansion was centered in the East and was

marked with the freshness of youth, the errors of the early here-
sies, the first great councils which refuted and defined, and those
amazing "Fathers of the church" whose sermons and writings
established a rich theological and liturgical tradition.

But then a second church arose. It was a church of the West,
with a more and more powerful center in Rome which would
be seriously challenged only by the Reformation. This church
of the "second era" was not lacking in organization and missionary zeal; it sent forth Jesuits, Franciscans, and many other
disciplined groups to bring the gospel to Africa, Asia, and Latin
America.

But now, just as we have a Third World, we also have a third
era and a third church. Fifty-eight percent of all Catholics now
live in the Third World. There are probably more Presbyterians
in Korea at this moment than there are in Scotland! The Catholic population of Mexico has doubled in twenty years. Brazil
has more bishops than any other country. The great majority of
Christians, Catholic or Protestant, no longer live in the Northern
Hemisphere.

While the cardinal archbishop of Paris worries about the day
when the predominant religion in France will be Islam, while the
cathedral of Cologne — with episcopal permission — is used as a
giant temporary mosque for Turkish "guest workers" on Moslem
holy days, while the seminaries of Ireland and Spain, formerly
crowded with students, remain empty, the number of Christians
grows rapidly in the Third World.

Although the Catholic Church in the United States has reg-
istered some increases in numbers (probably due to Mexican
immigration), the number of priests and nuns has been in de-
cline for some years. And among Methodists, Episcopalians, and
Presbyterians, the loss of members has been dramatic and frightening. But in Africa there has been an increase of one hundred
sixty thousand new Christians per day!

What does it mean? Since the Third World is an area of great
poverty and human misery, it means that most Christians are
poor, young, and dynamic. Theirs is a church of new initiatives.
It is a church of poor people restless to be free of the bondage
of hunger and sickness, unemployment and ignorance.

The poor, the great majority of people in the world, have
burst upon the scene and have claimed the church as their

own. As the church, especially since those important meetings at Medellín and Puebla, has made a "preferential option" for the poor, the poor have made an option for the church. More important than the sudden increase in priestly vocations in those places where the church has clearly identified with the poor is the emergence of a dynamic laity. They are eager and ready to carry on the work of the church — not because of priestly ordination but by virtue of their baptism.

As a Brazilian theologian has said:

It becomes a church where the valued sacraments are those which involve the laity — and the laity here, in the vast majority, are poor. It is basically the poor who are becoming the force within the church, making it a church of the poor majorities, a church of the world's dispossessed. We can say that this church is essentially democratic, while the church of the North is an aristocratic church marked by the clergy and middle-class movements.

Secondly, it is a church that assumes its responsibility within history, attempting to evolve the political, social and historical dimensions of the faith and doesn't limit itself to purely religious or sacramental aspects. It offers a liberating, social evangelization because it wants to transform society, contributing to the development of concrete historical projects. In Europe, it is a church that is mainly given over to the religious, the sacred; it is not very secular. These are the two characteristics that essentially differentiate the two churches: one is profoundly prophetic with a way of speaking that both responds to and denounces present day society; the other, the European church, is one that is at least partially victimized by ideology in that it allows itself to be manipulated by the values of the dominant ideologies.[1]

The church in so many places in the Third World is now clearly committed to the huge impoverished masses, the "little ones" who are found everywhere in Latin America, Africa, and Asia. As Leonardo Boff reminds us, "It is impossible to remove this church, through disciplinary means, from its immersion with the poor in their struggles. Withdrawal is impossible;

the church is not an army or football team that only follows orders from a captain or coach."

The "Christian base communities" that have appeared in great numbers in villages along the Amazon and in the poor *favelas* of Rio de Janeiro, and which even the pope now feels are not only useful but essential, have no intention of creating a schism and wish to be in communion with the universal church. But the Jesus whom they preach and accept has a different face and voice from the "therapeutic Christ" of easy consolations who blesses the "American way of life" through the voices of countless comfortable pastors and TV evangelists.

Rather it is Jesus the Liberator who is recognized and loved by the poor black, brown, and yellow people, the majority in today's Christian churches. It is the Jesus who said that he came to bring freedom to the captives and good news to the poor. For the masses of people who are becoming painfully aware of their exploitation by systems that have held them in bondage, these are words of hope and new life. Jesus has come to save us — to free us — as complete human beings, not merely as disembodied souls, and he must be followed and obeyed.

When Mary's Magnificat is read by the wretched of this earth, it takes on a rather different interpretation from that of subtle French theologians or cerebral German scripture scholars — not to mention North American ecclesiastical climbers. "The poor will be lifted up" is not a pious sentiment but an urgent promise!

However, even though Jesus Christ the Liberator may be deeply understood and his gospel of freedom sincerely welcomed in the slums of Lima and the shanty towns of South Africa, what of the land of Yuppies and big business? Is it true that the most difficult congregation a preacher can face are men between forty and fifty in a plush white suburb? Yet even as they grasp their professional prestige, their business success, and the ownership papers of the new BMW, they too need to hear of the Jesus who alone can make them free. Matthew at his counting table piled high with gold and silver coins, Nicodemus with his political clout and lofty position, Lazarus, Martha, and Mary in their comfortable suburban villa — all heard words that liberated and saved. Education and credit ratings will differ, but the poor and hungry, the ignorant and confused are waiting in the pews of every parish.

For many years I have been teaching preaching to the seminarians for diocesan priesthood. Many of them wish, I am sure, that I would wave some magic wand that would turn them into modern Augustines or Chrysostoms (or at least a new Fulton Sheen!). Surely there must be some set of rules, some wondrous textbook, that — if followed — will produce splendid preachers and splendid sermons.

Alas, preaching is something of an art and, like the arts of singing or acting, it has a history and a body of theory that can be learned. Like other arts it is best taught through practice, criticism, exposure to styles and possibilities. A preacher who is both learned and creative (qualities that are not always found together) would seem to be essential today for really good preaching. But all of this is still not enough!

Paul says that Timothy has been sent as "God's coworker in the gospel of Christ, to establish you and encourage your faith" (1 Thess. 3:2). Timothy and every other Christian preacher is to be the "coworker" of God! God's collaborator and cooperator![2] The preacher's calling is both noble and risky. A sinner surely, he or she cooperates with God "in the gospel of Christ." Every Christian is called to holiness, but for the one who collaborates with God himself in the divine work of liberation and salvation, holiness and a life of prayer and charity take on a special urgency.

We preachers will be able to "talk about Jesus" with passion and love when we know him, when we stay close to him, when we allow him to free us and challenge us. Tepid "talk about Jesus" comes from tepid people. The word of God, alive and active in the holy scriptures, will also be alive and active in the preaching of those who pray and who care — truly care — about the Lord and his people.

"Behold, I have put my words in your mouth" (Jer. 1:9). But Christ not only had God's word in his mouth, he also did God's work. His preaching was invariably linked with obvious signs that show forth and confirm the truth of what he said. He teaches, but then he "validates" his preaching with a material sign, concrete and vivid. For example, the healing of the man with the unclean spirit follows his teaching in the temple (Mark 1:21–27; Matt. 4:23). He not only commands his apostles to preach but also to heal: "Whenever you enter a town...heal the sick in it and say to them, 'The kingdom of God has drawn near you'" (Luke 10:8f.). These signs, these dramatic acts of Jesus and his followers, confirm and "actualize" their preaching of the kingdom. The diseased and the possessed experience the power of the word of God; unclean spirits are exorcized by the commands of Jesus (Matt. 8:16; Luke 4:36); he speaks and "even the winds and sea obey him" (Mark 4:41f.); in fact, he even forgives sins (Mark 2:7). No one could ever accuse Jesus of being a mere "man of words," for he did many "signs and wonders."

It may no longer be necessary for the church to establish hospitals and leper colonies, orphanages and colleges. The state has moved into many areas with enormous funding and armies of social workers. But a church that no longer does "signs and wonders," that no longer heals the broken and lifts up the fallen, but only preaches and teaches will lose the *dynamis*, the power of the word. Pity and service for the least of the Lord's brothers and sisters and proclamation of the gospel are the Christian's double imperative.

It is our noble task to go into the pulpits of our churches and through the world "talking about Jesus." But it is also our challenge and our joy to do — in our feeble, limited, and highly imperfect way — some "signs and wonders." Jesus preached, he healed, and he liberated. He came not only with a message about God but he offered true participation in the divine life. He responded with love and compassion to the needs of the sick and the sinful, to the hungry crowds on the hillside or the weeping women of Jerusalem. For Jesus, there was never a conflict between "words" and "works," for they supported and validated each other. Indeed, the word of God leads to action. "My mother and my brethren are those who hear the word of God and do it" (Luke 8:20).

And a preacher? Can he or she do anything other than speak the word of God and do it? For, as Dietrich Bonhoeffer said during World War II: "Only he who cries out for the Jews dare permit himself to sing Gregorian chant." Today only he or she who fights for justice for Arabs in Israel, for blacks in South Africa, and for the poor in El Salvador; who works for peace and hope amid violence and despair in our own cities; who is serious about the problems of education, drugs, guns, and racism, dares stand and say the holy words. Yes, there is a need for a fresh and powerful preaching. But there is also a need for a few startling new signs and wonders. Talk about Jesus should move both preacher and congregation to doing what Jesus wants done today.

• 3 •

RISING EXPECTATIONS

I have just heard of a pastor of a suburban parish who found it necessary to resign. There were probably many factors leading to his decision, but I suspect that one important reason was a recent letter he received from the seventh- and eighth-grade pupils. They stated that they would no longer attend church on Sunday until his sermons improved! One wonders how much their parents had to do with this letter which so devastated this pastor; it certainly doesn't sound like the sort of thing some grammar-school kids would do on their own. However, the idea of children judging his sermons and threatening to boycott the church until he came up to their standards could shake any preacher's peace of mind!

This may be a unique horror story, but many people today feel it is open season all year long for shooting at the poor soul who dares to climb into the pulpit. More than a few ministers and priests have received phone calls or letters (some signed and some anonymous) with some very negative comments about their preaching abilities. Perhaps parishioners in colonial times also had some bitter and angry feelings about the long and dreary sermons they experienced, but their hostility remained latent. Today it all spills out into the open.

It would seem valuable, therefore, to ask people what they think about the present phenomena of preaching. I admit that I depend more on impressionistic findings than on scientific data resulting from studies of sociologists and psychologists. However, as valuable as their statistics are and as much as we need this type of controlled research for homiletic studies, it may be that samples of receiver response will add another dimension to our "phenomenology of preaching" which a listing of percentages could not do.

This writer asked the congregations at two different parishes to mail in a note or card giving their feelings about the sermons that they hear. The first was in a middle-class suburb on the edge of Chicago. Here the congregation was meeting in an auditorium-gymnasium for Sunday liturgy around an improvised altar. Music was provided by guitars and the hymns were in the folk-music style. From three hundred to four hundred people attended, and a spirit of community seemed to have already developed at the time the request for "feedback" was made.

About forty letters, cards, and notes were mailed in after a single invitation. When we remember that not more than four hundred people heard this invitation and that many of these were small children, this response seems to be very good and to indicate a strong desire to express their ideas on this subject, even to the extent of sitting down to write a letter, buy a stamp, and to go the mailbox.

The second church was in Chicago. It is a very large middle-income parish on the North Side with many German, Hungarian, Irish, and Italian members. The hymns and liturgy were traditional, and the response to the survey was poor in view of the large number of people at these services, celebrated in an enormous church building. It could be expected, of course, that the many foreign-born parishioners would hesitate to write a letter in a strange language.

There was little doubt that the men and women who wrote were concerned about preaching. It seemed to be the first time that they had ever been asked their opinions on this subject, and they were grateful to have the opportunity to express themselves. Many seemed to be looking for sermons that "speak of things common to us all," those that deal with "modern everyday trials and tribulations, the teachings of God as part of our everyday world."

Young people wanted sermons that were "geared expressly for us teens," and felt that they had been neglected as a group. An older woman wanted the sermon to be "a friendly conversation with religious overtones." A married man wanted "feedback" on the sermons to be written on cards and placed in suggestion boxes near the doors. A young father of three children felt that "future sermons should be concerned with the themes of the Gospels, applied to present everyday living." Again and again there were pleas that sermons be "spoken in down-to-earth language everyone understands" and "always be up-to-date."

A couple engaged to be married wrote, "We would like to hear more sermons about man's responsibility to his fellow man, rather than about the mechanics of worship." An older woman asked for a sermon that would not be the "usual continuous repetition of catechism" but rather "a way of bringing God's word into today's way of life — our way of life." Preaching was looked upon as a way in which we begin to understand God and feel he understands us. A number of people looked for a word of hope in the sermon.

One woman remarked: "A thorough course in speech would certainly improve many priests. What good to us are their exalted sentiments if they can't convey them effectively?" There was a strong feeling that many sermons were too negative and that the preacher "talked down" to the congregation. Many felt bored and yet helpless to do anything to improve the sermons they hear. Someone asked, "Why drag on rehashing and padding and repeating and rephrasing what has been said before for another ten minutes?" Preachers were reminded that they should "give the listener credit for some sense!"

Although these letters represented only a limited slice of American Catholic life, they do illustrate both the interest that many have in religion and in preaching and also a willingness to comment in a critical way. Some of the letters were, in fact, very pointed, very outspoken, and deeply concerned about the quality of Catholic preaching.

There have, of course, always been complaints from Christians about the sermons they had to endure. But it is only in the last few years that preaching seems to cause such acute pain that many churchgoers no longer solve the problem of the bad preacher by quietly dozing as he drones on, but are rather impelled to speak out against a punishment they do not deserve.

Have sermons become progressively worse through the years? We have no reason to say so. If anything, there seems to have been some improvement if we compare today's typically direct and simple homilies with the verbose and artificial preaching that was not uncommon some years ago. We could judge from the text alone that today's shorter sentences and more simple syntax are better suited to oral communication than a good deal of the complicated literary wanderings that passed for preaching in the past. And when a preacher of the "old school" gets up to orate, face florid, voice and gestures full of melodrama, we can only feel that today's "conversational style" has been a giant step forward. It is not that the quality of preaching has been dropping; it is rather that the quality of the listeners has been rising so rapidly.

Today's Christians are not necessarily better than their parents. They are, however, better educated. They come to church bringing a background of formal and informal education that their grandparents and even their parents could not begin to understand. Grandfather may well have come from Europe with the equivalent of a fourth-grade education. Father and mother may have graduated from high school and even have worked their way through a semester or two of college. But now the American dream has come to include a bachelor's degree, and today's young Christian man and woman may already be planning to send their children through graduate school.

Even today's immigrant from Ireland, Poland, the Philippines, and Italy may skip the tenements of the inner city and quickly find a place in the trades or in industry. It is only in Spanish-speaking areas and in some — but certainly not all — black neighborhoods that the pastor can expect a congregation of very limited formal education. The younger generation must stay in high school until the age of sixteen, and the more ambitious receive a diploma from high school and take some college courses in night school. Puerto Rican and Mexican teenagers soon learn from subway-station posters that education is very much a part of the American way of life in which they want to share.

And certainly, in almost every case, the new suburban parishes around the country are made up of educated people who are committed to still higher standards of education, culture, and success for their children. For some, it is no longer a question of sending their sons and daughters to college but of choosing between Princeton and Dartmouth. When we consider that few bishops in the United States have parents who graduated from college, and many suburban pastors are the proud sons of policemen and streetcar conductors, it is clear how rapidly the church is changing. Large numbers of its people have avidly accepted middle-class values, one of the most important of which is education.

But the hours of classroom instruction and assigned reading that modern students accept as their right and their key to success form only a part of their education. Adults and children spend many hundreds of hours as docile disciples of the "tube." Informal education goes on and on.

Most of this massive program of informal education is sophisticated, sometimes cynical, but seldom bland and uninteresting. The cardinal sin in the mass media is to be tedious. The unpardonable offense in advertising is to be ignored. Into the church on Sunday morning come men and women who have spent a good part of the past week, in fact a good part of their lives, under the tutelage of these skilled and potent teachers.

Our parishioners, therefore, are not only better educated, they are also more critical. Their education, both formal and informal, has helped them to become so. The preacher of only a few years ago expected and received the assent and approval of his congregation for almost everything he or she said. This may have been more external than internal, but the fact is that hundreds of sermons might be given with never a negative response. "Pastor is always right" seemed to be the motto of the people in the pews as they nodded in agreement to whatever was said from the pulpit. After all, with very few exceptions, the minister or priest was the best-educated man in the neighborhood. The clergy formed a sort of sacred, educated, ruling caste, with a special garb, honorific titles, and unique lifestyle. It took a person of extraordinary temerity to question even the *obiter dicta* in a sermon.

But this has changed. The modern Christian, listening to the Sunday sermon, may be quite young (one of every two people in the United States is under twenty-five), fairly well educated and opinionated, and was probably subjected to a torrent of language from many fluent sources since he or she was able to sit in front of the TV set. He or she sees no contradiction in being a "believer" and a "critic" at the same time and rather quickly sees through a preacher to expose his ignorance, his lack of empathy, and his pomposity. Today the clergy must often stand condemned when their knowledge is deficient and when their coldness and lack of feeling are compared to the warmth and personal charm of the news broadcaster or weatherman! They are made to take their place in the lineup with the other speakers, and the comparison is frequently not flattering.

New distinctions are being made between the person and the message which were impossible a few years ago. The pastor must prove himself as a person; the preacher must prove himself as a speaker. The younger generation will accept nothing else, and they find the "built-in" prestige that all clergy formerly enjoyed quite incredible. Even older people have come to resent the paternalism that they remember well. They now have a new sensitivity to whatever reveals a lack of sincere respect for them.

A young layman can say:

> In tone, assumption, stance, language, the act of communication defines a human attitude and shapes a human reality. Here the converging disciplines of literary criticism, politics, linguistic philosophy, criticism of cultural media meet to form one of the most significant bodies of thinking in our time. What kind of communication, then, is set up in the average sermon? What are the human implications behind it, what version of relationships does it suggest? What is the nature of the language we use in the church, in sermons, prayers, hymns? Is this democratic language, language that establishes respect and equality? Or how far can we make a parallel between the attitudes of the sermon-makers toward their audiences and the attitudes of the admen and controllers of media? How far, in both cases, is there an easy assumption about the "masses," who need to be chastised, goaded, bribed, mothered? What we are looking for in society is a kind of communication that will establish community between men, as in the liturgy Christ is established at the focus of a number of converging human communications.[1]

Here is a new awareness of the power of language, a resentment when it is used improperly, and a need for sincere words that speak out clearly and honestly, without the hidden hooks of the commercial copy. For as much as the Christian is forced to admire the imaginative daring and high style of the admen, he finds their manipulation of language and people especially repugnant in the guise of religion. He or she has suffered enough from the "hidden persuaders" and the political propagandists. When their techniques are adopted for a holy purpose, he spontaneously feels that it is only a new and more abhorrent kind of "paternalism." Is the preacher any less a bully if he conceives of himself as a subtle manipulator of the human heart and mind, a clever and professional "adman of the sacred" who exploits what he has learned of the social psychology of groups to persuade and control "for the greater glory of God?" Brainwashing "in the service of Christ" sounds blasphemous. "The fullest consequence of communication is respect for equality of being; to know a man in his depth is to know that I can have no ultimate power over him, without mutual damage. If the full implications of this are seen, we can perhaps go beyond liberal paternalism to a real community."[2]

The Christian, especially the new critical Christian, has wanted the spoken word not only to build community among people but to be a means of establishing communion with Jesus Christ. He has wanted at least some of the preaching that he hears to be a prayer, that is, to bring him to contact with Jesus and his heavenly Father. Although, of his own prayers, he might have to say with the king in *Hamlet:*

> My words fly up, my thoughts remain below.
> Words without thoughts never to heaven go.
> (*Hamlet*, III, iii, 97–98)

He still hopes that at least the preaching word will reach out to him, drawing him closer to his brothers and sisters and to his Savior, freeing him from his isolation, the coldness of his heart, and the heaviness of his thoughts. So often he has been disappointed.

And this is unquestionably part of the present "crisis of preaching." Rising expectations on the part of a more critical and sophisticated audience have outstripped the preaching performance. In the world, language has become, as Stuart Chase says, a "tyranny of words." The very means to create and preserve community has become a confusing obstacle. In the church, the sermon, instead of being a point of contact between God and man, an encounter in faith, hope, and love, has proved to be not merely a negative and empty experience but also a positive hindrance for many Christians of good will.

At the very time when personalism and humanistic psychology are asserting the importance of human relationships, at the very time when client-oriented theories and creative expression have become prominent, the preacher, alone and aloof, may continue to stand in his pulpit for a "Sunday speech." Though ecclesiastical theorists may write endlessly about the homily as a communal experience, the new critical Christian often does *not* experience community in it. To talk about community that is, perhaps, never experienced is an unreal and useless exercise. Self-knowledge, new and better attitudes, love of neighbor — if these come at all, they seem to come not because of the sermon but in spite of it. For many, they are discovered in the dynamics of a basic encounter and relationship between individuals in a completely secular setting. During the sermon, both the preacher's and the listeners' defenses and façades are held high. There is no real opportunity to relate directly on a feeling basis with anyone since there is obviously little freedom and a great deal of structure. No one is allowed to feel safe enough or accepted enough to come into a basic encounter with other members of the group. The preacher remains isolated in his pulpit in a web of words and the people sit isolated, unhappy, and increasingly frustrated in their benches.

Certainly this is not what the Lord had in mind when he told his disciples to go into the whole world with "good news" to free us from fear, slavery, and sin. Our "high-tech" world certainly does not need a computer in the pulpit, the hard plastic rhetoric of a television "personality," a narcissistic indulgence in complexity and irrelevance. Like every age, it will find communion only in the simple, the beautiful, and the true.

A Navy chaplain recently invited me to Sunday brunch and a tour of the aircraft carrier *Carl Vinson*. It must be the biggest and the most expensive ship ever built in the history of the world! Its nuclear power could keep it sailing the seas nonstop for fifteen years; its food lockers can feed six thousand men for six months; its one hundred aircraft could destroy the largest cities; its computer systems are the most advanced. And each Sunday its three Christian chaplains help the "spoken Christ" be present to its crew. The men before them (there are no woman yet on ships of war) are certainly not the fishermen of Galilee or the sailors of ancient Corinth. They are young men from a culture that tells them that the night belongs to one brand of beer, the weekends belong to another, and "Joy" is the name of a perfume! Their minds and imaginations have been formed by hours of television, illustrated magazines, and the latest songs. Many, perhaps most of them, are the sons of broken homes. Some have vivid memories of drunken parents, family violence, gangs, and drugs. The great majority are "unchurched." Indeed the ship's chapel would be far too small to hold them if more than a small minority showed up for Sunday services. But some do come! What are their expectations?

When all is said and done, don't they want to meet Jesus? Don't they, like all the rest of us, want to know that the Lord is present once again in this crazy and confusing world? That he challenges us, encourages us, and saves us from despair and death?

On a nuclear warship, in prison or hospital chapel, in Bolivian village or French cathedral, in the heart of a noisy, dirty, and dangerous city or in the suburban sprawl, Jesus Christ would be present to his people. He would invite them, heavily burdened, to come to him, calling them to love one another and even suggesting that they be "holy as your heavenly Father is holy." A strong and dangerous message, surely, but also some eagerly awaited "good news."

Jesus took a risk, He entrusted his message to the limitations of language and the sounds of the human voice. As the eucharistic Christ is dependent on humble food and drink, so the "spoken Christ" depends on the oral interpretation of his story and the preaching that flows from it.

The Word of God is met in words. Language, so mysterious yet so common, so potent yet so obviously frail, so rich yet so frequently ambiguous, so noble yet so often abused, becomes a way for Christ to be present.

The Son of God became vulnerable and close to us through his incarnation; now the "spoken Christ" comes again and again, ready to meet us in our thoughts and imaginations through human communication.

He comes into our midst through words. Humble words. Beautiful words. Words of wonder and power. Once he took our flesh and entered our human history. Now he takes our language and enters our consciousness. In fact, a meeting with the "spoken Christ" precedes recognizing him in any of the other modes of his loving presence. "Faith comes through hearing." Unless the Lord is encountered first of all through the gospel proclaimed among us, it is quite possible that we will not see him at all.

Will we ever recognize him disguised and hidden behind the vacant stare of the prisoner, the gaunt face of the hungry, and the unhealthy skin of the diseased? Will we come to understand that he continues to bless, nourish, and heal in those sacred signs we call "sacraments"? Will we become reverently and happily aware that he truly dwells within us? Only if, like the two disciples at Emmaus, we first hear the gospel word and realize that "our hearts were burning within us as he spoke to us on the way."

· 4 ·

THE NECESSARY WORD

The "demythologizing" of the clergy, pope, bishops, ministers, and priests has proceeded at a fast pace, gaining further momentum from the solemnly irrelevant pronouncements and repressive tactics of some clerics. This dramatic loss of both Protestant and Catholic episcopal and priestly prestige, the incongruity of autocratic outmoded attitudes, the hollowness of feudal and regal pretensions, the obvious theological and communicative incompetencies — all these the "new" laity know, and they begin to wonder if they still want or need a preacher in the pulpit.

The pastor serves a purpose, the layman reasons, when he functions as counselor or as liturgist, but his role as preacher no longer seems important or even necessary in this era of mass media and lay leadership.

The preaching of evangelization seems better done through books and magazines, television and movies, and through the testimony of laity among other laity, joining together in the building up of the kingdom. The incarnation of Christ among us seems best announced in an incarnational way, that is, by those who speak from their deep involvement in the "secular city" and who share lay responsibilities.

The preaching of catechesis has been accomplished for a long time now by lay teachers. Educational psychology, audio-visual aids, the mass media, and sociological research are tools for expert teaching of Christian doctrine that can be used by the laity. In many parishes, the pastors have been happy to hand over the preaching of catechesis to others who are better trained and more effective teachers of both children and adults.

The preaching of the homily, however, remains a clerical preserve, but here too there are a growing number of laity who
would prefer the silence of a Quaker meeting, the "still, inner voice" to the "God talk" of the pastor. There is a feeling
that some moments of reflection, a "going apart" with Christ in
private prayers, might be better than the "professional pieties"
uttered by bored or inarticulate clergymen.

> Talk of God that lacks authenticity, that has become empty
> and powerless, spells disintegration to faith and thought.
> On this, whether pious or not, all are fundamentally agreed.
> And hopefully the non-believers will not be the sole ad-
> vocates of thought. Whoever takes the holiness of God
> seriously should make certain that no one is more con-
> scientious than he in the use of words. That has always
> been so, but it has also always been questioned. Talk of
> God is word at its most demanding, because it demands
> pure faith. For this reason such talk is always in danger of
> becoming presumptuous and incredible. . . .
>   Far more than is normally realized, our customary talk
> of God — dull sermons and pious words which have no
> bearing on reality and cause us no further thought — has
> become empty, producing a slow disintegration. The con-
> sequences of this are not by any means to be found only
> in the religious realm, but also are considerable outside of
> it — namely, in the devaluation of words in general, the
> debilitation of the responsible use of language.[1]

Since God dwells in glory, outside of our experience; since
communion with him is a mystery; and since his love, his mercy,
and his justice are so splendid that even laborious reflection,
the genius of the poet, and the insights of the mystic cannot
do a suitable job of translation for us, there is the temptation
to consider all talk of him as somewhat improper. Only silence
would seem to be appropriate. The preacher becomes more than
an annoyance; he appears as an intolerable intrusion.

So, too, the very language of Christian proclamation seems
to sound more and more like a private language for the chosen
few. In the bigger world outside the sanctuary, it sounds merely
quaint and old-fashioned, with no real link to the world of secu-

larized culture, politics, science, and economics. It is made up of
English nouns and verbs, but in fact it remains a "cult" language,
as dead as ancient Latin or Greek. It may be brought out, with
the incense and vestments, for use at weddings and funerals and
even for a short time on Sundays. Its anthropomorphism seems
incomprehensible in an age of scientific empiricism; its diction
of love and hope seems irreconcilable with the real catastrophes
of hate and despair in our lifetime.

These objections, although they are certainly real and abra-
sive at the present time, are not at all new in the history of
preaching. One may hear echoes in the present complaints that
go back through the Enlightenment and the Reformation to New
Testament times and to the days of the Hebrew prophets. It may
be small consolation to the contemporary Christian, but preaching has sounded unreal and empty before. Preachers in the past
have often failed to translate the word of God into the word
of man. More than once a preacher has been a stumbling block
and a scandal.

The Christian religion, however, continues to be a religion of
preaching. As necessary as silent prayer may be, Christianity is
dedicated to announcing the "good news" to the nations through
the spoken word. Even today, the poor, materially or spiritually,
must have the gospel preached to them or the church would not
be faithful to its commission.

The fact remains that Christians are those who follow "Jesus
of Nazareth, who was a prophet mighty in word and deed before
God and all the people" (Luke 24:19). Jesus applied to himself
the words of Isaiah: "The Spirit of the Lord is upon me, because
he has appointed me to preach good news to the poor ... to proclaim the acceptable year of the Lord" (Luke 4:18–19). Matthew,
giving a short review of the work that Jesus did in Galilee, put
his preaching in the first place: "And he went about all Galilee,
teaching in their synagogues and preaching the gospel of the
kingdom and healing every disease and every infirmity among
the people" (Matt. 4:23).

Christ did not remain silent about God. Indeed, "no man
ever spoke like this man!" (John 7:46). "Speaking" was characteristic of Jesus; he declared at his trial: "I have spoken openly
to the world; I have always taught in synagogues and in the temple, where all Jews come together; I have said nothing secretly.

Why do you ask me? Ask those who have heard me, what I said to them; they know what I said" (John 18:20–21). He was a "witness" giving "testimony": "For this I was born, and for this I have come into the world, to bear witness to the truth" (John 18:37).

Here, in the preaching of Christ, is the beginning of salvation for faithful Christians. The word of God was spoken among men by a man: the poor had the gospel preached to them. Christ was a preacher, and it is this which Peter noted when he began his own preaching to the Gentiles: "You know the word which he [God] sent to Israel, preaching good news of peace by Jesus Christ" (Acts 10:36).

Christ, then, called others to hand on what they had heard from him. The author of the Epistle to the Hebrews said: "For this deliverance was first announced through the lips of the Lord himself; those who heard him confirmed it to us, and God added his testimony by signs, by miracles, by manifold works of power, and by distributing the gifts of the Holy Spirit at his own will" (2:3–4). His message of salvation would be continued by those whom he called. The apostles and the disciples were sent out as preachers. "... go and proclaim the kingdom of God" (Luke 9:60). "Go into all the world and preach the gospel to the whole creation" (Mark 16:15). "Then he opened their minds to understand the scriptures and said to them: 'Thus it is written, that the Christ should suffer and on the third day rise from the dead, and that repentance and forgiveness of sins should be preached in his name to all nations, beginning from Jerusalem. You are witnesses of these things'" (Luke 24:45–48). What Christ has begun was to be continued "in his name" by the preaching of those sent forth as witnesses.

The apostles were depicted above all as preachers: "And every day in the temple and at home they did not cease teaching and preaching Jesus as the Christ" (Acts 5:42). And when there was danger that they would become too busy about other things, deacons were chosen, since "it is not right that we should give up preaching the word of God to serve tables.... But we will devote ourselves to prayer and to the ministry of the word" (Acts 6:2–4). They seem to have felt a compulsion to preach: "For we cannot but speak of what we have seen and heard" (Acts 4:20).

Paul preached and looked upon this apostolate as priestly service: "...the grace given me by God to be a minister of Christ Jesus to the Gentiles in the priestly service of the gospel of God, so that the offering of the Gentiles may be acceptable, sanctified by the Holy Spirit" (Rom. 15:15–16). For Paul, this task took priority over giving the sacrament of baptism: "For Christ did not send me to baptize but to preach the gospel" (1 Cor. 1:17). There was a "setting apart" — a call for the purpose of preaching: "But when he who had set me apart before I was born, and called me through his grace, was pleased to reveal his Son to me, in order that I might preach him among the Gentiles..." (Gal. 1:15–16).

The apostles were made strong by the words of Christ: "He who hears you hears me, and he who rejects you rejects me, and he who rejects me rejects him who sent me" (Luke 10:16). They spoke, therefore, with divine authority. Paul could write: "And we also thank God constantly for this, that when you received the word of God which you heard from us, you accepted it not as the word of men but as what it really is, the word of God, which is at work in you believers" (1 Thess. 2:13).

But Paul, in his turn, wanted to hand down what had been entrusted to him to other generations. The doctrine of Christ must be maintained: "I command you because you remember me in everything and maintain the traditions even as I have delivered them to you" (1 Cor. 11:2). Timothy was made a link in the chain of preaching; Paul told him: "You then, my son, be strong in the grace that is in Christ Jesus, and what you have heard from me before many witnesses entrust to faithful men who will be able to reach others also" (2 Tim. 2:1–2). "O Timothy, guard what has been entrusted to you" (1 Tim. 6:20).

In the New Testament, therefore, there can be no doubt that the preacher is indispensable in the plan of salvation: "But how are men to call upon him [Christ] in whom they have not believed? And how are they to believe in him of whom they have never heard? And how are they to hear without a preacher? And how can men preach unless they are sent?" (Rom. 10:14–15). There must be preachers and they must have a mission. Both the doctrine and the ministry of the Lord are to be handed down by the apostles to their successors. Paul could, in fact, say of these preachers near the end of his own life: "Their voice has gone out to all the earth, and their words to the ends of the world" (Rom. 10:18).

It has been the constant teaching of the church that the bishops, above all, have received the responsibility for the continued preaching of Christ in the world. Pope John XXIII said that the hierarchy's first and gravest responsibility is to assure the continuity and presence of the word of God in the world by preaching and teaching of revealed truth.[2] They must make sure that the preaching of Christ, of Peter and Paul, of Titus and Timothy and Barnabas extends down to their century and their people.

In the rite for the consecration of a bishop this is made specific. The consecrator asks the bishop-elect in the examination: "We ask you, beloved brother, in true charity, whether you are willing in so far as in you lies, to conform your judgment to the teaching of holy scriptures?" His teaching must be the teaching of Christ; his judgment must conform to the higher judgment of the scriptures.

"Are you willing, by word and example, to teach what you have learned from the sacred scripture to the people for whose service you are to be consecrated?" He does not become a bishop for himself but rather to serve others as a preacher of the word. The open book of the gospels is placed upon the neck and shoulders of the bishop-elect to symbolize his call to be a servant of the word with the core burden of proclaiming the gospel. The book of the Gospels remains on his shoulders during the conferral of orders, while the consecrator and coconsecrators successively impose hands on the head of the bishop-elect.

As the consecrator anoints the head of the new bishop with oil he prays: "Thanks to your gift, may his coming to tell of peace, to announce good news, be welcome. Endow him, Lord, with the ministry of reconciliation in word and deed, and sanction it by signs and wonders. Let his message, his preaching, depend on no persuasive language devised of human wisdom, but rather on the proof he gives of spiritual power."

And when the consecrator hands the book of the Gospels to the newly consecrated bishop he says: "Take this gospel, go and preach to the people entrusted to your care; mighty is God to enrich you with his grace: he who lives and reigns forever and ever. Amen." At this sacred time and in these solemn words the faith of the church concerning the mission of preaching is made clear. The bishops have received the mission to preach. It is a serious obligation that they may not neglect.

But although the church makes the bishops responsible for the continued preaching of the word of God, it is clear that they cannot do this preaching alone. Since the days of the apostles, others have been chosen to share in the preaching of the gospel. Deacons were chosen, first of all as helpers in social care and works of charity, but soon Stephen and Philip were joining in the preaching of the church. As the Christians grew in number, the bishops came to share more and more of their responsibilities with elders, deacons, and others. In the ordination of priests and deacons, a share in the ministry of proclaiming the gospel is officially given.

Priests and deacons, therefore, are called to extend and multiply the works of the bishop. The fullness of the bishop's pastoral responsibilities and ministry could be divided in any one of a number of ways. The ordination of priests and deacons indicates the bishop's need for helpers and is their official entry into his ministry of the word. But the bishop may call others to assist in various ways. There can be many ministries for both priests and laity. Laity who already announce the word of God in the scriptural readings could also share in the ministry of preaching. The pastor, however, the official representative of the bishop in his parish community, must see that the gospel is preached, even though he may not always do that preaching himself. As a "good shepherd" and as president of the community of Christians in a given place, he must direct the preaching of the gospel and be officially responsible for the telling of the story of Jesus.

But just as the bishop needs priests, the priest needs helpers if the Christian story is to be effectively told and the drama played out.

As Michael Schmaus has indicated, the whole church both preaches and listens to the word.[3] Every baptized person has an inescapable responsibility to preach the word. St. Paul insisted on the importance of prophetic preaching at the meetings of the Christian community. Anyone who was there could be used as an instrument of God. There was not to be, however, disorder and religious fanaticism.

So if the whole congregation is assembled and all are using the "strange tongues" of ecstasy, and some uninstructed persons or unbelievers should enter, will they not think you are mad? But if all are uttering prophecies, the visitor, when he enters, hears from everyone something that searches his conscience and brings conviction, and the secrets of his heart are laid bare. So he will fall down and worship God, crying, "God is certainly among you!" (1 Cor. 14:23–25).

It would be wrong therefore merely to divide the church into two parties or castes, that of the teachers and that of the students. Every member of the church must believe and, since faith comes by hearing, as St. Paul said, all members of the Church, ordained ministers and the laity are listeners, students of the word of God. So, too, everyone is called on to give witness to his faith, to confess that Christ is the Lord, to preach the gospel.

... the office of teaching oversteps all distinctions. It embraces all the members of the Church in a single body. Not everyone teaches by the same title and obligation. The differences rest on foundations laid by Christ himself. But everyone shares in the Church's duty to preach. The task is completely universal, and the duty we have in common must not be forgotten or despised for any reason connected with the differences between us. This common task differentiates the adherents to the Church from everyone else. And according to scripture, this line of demarcation is more important than any within the Church.[4]

Just as every Christian may share in the celebration of the Eucharist, the central act of our religion, so also every Christian joins in the preaching of Christ. It has been so from the beginning. The invisible representative of Jesus, the Holy Spirit, filled about a hundred and twenty people at Pentecost and inspired them to speak in the streets of Jerusalem, "preaching the wonderful acts of God" to both the natives and foreign visitors. The power of prophetic speech belonged to all the people of God and not just to the apostles.

When many people were amazed and perplexed at this, Peter stood up with the Eleven and addressed them:

Fellow Jews, and all you who live in Jerusalem, mark this and give me a hearing. These men are not drunk, as you imagine; for it is only nine in the morning. No, this is what the prophet spoke of: "God says, 'This will happen in the last days: I will pour out upon everyone a portion of my spirit; and your sons and daughters shall prophesy; your young men shall see visions, and your old men shall dream dreams. Yes, I will endue even my slaves, both men and women, with a portion of my spirit, and they shall prophesy'" (Acts 2:14–18).

No distinction is made here between apostles and the others, between men and women, between old and young. All will have a portion of God's spirit.

The New Testament constantly comes back to the conviction that all Christians are called to be witnesses to Christ, "salt of the earth," "light of the world," "a light that will shine to all that are in the house." They are expected to give encouragement to one another at the assemblies (Heb. 10:23–25). But it is the Holy Spirit who will choose those who will perform particular acts of preaching, giving the proper charisma as he wills. It is true that the preaching of these chosen ones should conform to the teaching of the apostles and the traditions that they handed down. But also, St. Paul declared, they were not to be silenced: "Do not stifle inspiration, and do not despise prophetic utterances but bring them all to the test and then keep what is good in them and avoid the bad of whatever kind" (1 Thess. 5:19–22).

Dr. Schmaus remarks: "Baptism itself gives every baptized person a general commission to preach, and in this baptismal commissioning it is God himself who bestows the authorization. The call to join the people of God given in baptism carries with it the capability as well as the privilege and duty of preaching within the hierarchical order of the Church established by Christ."[5] Although a new existential relationship with Christ is effected by ordination, the fundamental obligation to proclaim the gospel came with Christian baptism. Building on this foundation, ordination adds a special responsibility and pastoral

authority. It does not necessarily bring with it additional prophetic charisma. And as everyone should know who has looked
into the history of the church, ordination into the hierarchy of
pastoral and magisterial authorities does not necessarily mean
an entrance into a hierarchy of holiness.

The call to preach the word of Christ, therefore, can be heard
by all Christians. Preaching is a ministry that goes back to Jesus
and his apostles and is fundamental to Christianity, a missionary church, a church for those "on the way." Silence, of course,
is needed for prayer and reflection, and periods of silence are
necessary even in public worship. In a climate of silence and
attention the word of God that has been heard may then penetrate deeply into the human spirit. But silence cannot replace
preaching. The gospel must still be spoken in our language by
human preachers so that Christ may be obeyed and a church-
community formed among men and women.

We can expect a much greater participation of lay people
in the ministry of the word. The clerical monopoly on preaching was unknown in the early church because early Christianity
was a lay movement, open to all. The controls and restrictions,
the nervous emphasis on the necessity for a *missio canonica*,
and finally the almost complete elimination of lay preaching are
now seen as the result of disputes between the parish clergy and
wandering friars in the Middle Ages, fears of heresy, and a general lack of learning and culture among both clergy and laity.
By insisting that no one preach in his diocese without his ex-
plicit permission, and by refusing to give "faculties to preach"
to the more ignorant or doctrinally dangerous, a bishop could
try to save his people from confusion and exploitation, from
being sold indulgences from the pulpit, from heresy and super-
stition. It was difficult to control the vagrant monks and friars
who traveled from town to town. False doctrines grew up like
weeds among an illiterate and credulous people. The laity were
often thought to be already contaminated by heresy and so were
not to be trusted. Their prophetic voice was legally muted and
two separate classes, teachers and pupils, evolved in the church.

Today, of course, the voice of the laity can again be heard,
even in the pulpit. In this age of an educated and vocal laity, it
was inevitable that the old prohibitions would be relaxed; the
dangers of the past are not always the dangers of the present. The

apostolic layperson is no longer considered a potential danger and a cryptoheretic by many pastors but rather a helper in the enormous task of preaching the gospel. It is necessary that he or she once again take part in building up the Christian community through the spoken word. Both men and women from the laity are now asked to preach, but usually outside of the structure of the liturgy.

But there must be a preacher! Someone must help the listener to have a living encounter with God. The mystery of Christ is realized in us through the words of a speaker like the rest of us. Christ continues to work over the centuries through the medium of human language. He borrows the voice of the preacher. Such is the Christian belief.

It was the great St. Teresa of Avila who said:

Now Christ has no body on earth but yours;
Now Christ has no hands here on earth but yours.
Yours are the eyes through which his compassion looks out
    on the world;
Yours are the feet which carry him now on his way;
Yours are the hands which touch his people today.

We might properly add a second verse to Teresa's:

Now Christ has no voice here on earth but yours;
Now Christ has no words to be heard but yours.
Yours is the voice that speaks to the captives of freedom
    and hope;
Yours are the words which promise the wounded a cure;
Yours is the voice that brings good news to the poor.[6]

• 5 •

THE RISE AND FALL OF THE PULPIT

Probably no one would deny that Jesus Christ, at least on occasion, gave speeches. Although the New Testament scholars argue about just how much of the Sermon on the Mount, as we now have it recorded, was actually given at one time and one particular place, there seems to be little doubt that Christ did speak to large numbers of people.

Another vivid scene from the New Testament shows Christ making Peter's boat into an improvised "pulpit" in order to speak to the many people who were pressing down to the very edge of the water to hear him. He asked Peter to push out a bit from the shore, and then, from the fishing boat, he gave a speech to the crowds on the beach.

Although there were no loudspeakers to amplify his voice in the open air, the magnetism of Christ as a speaker drew five thousand people out into the desert. The gospel makes it clear that Christ's audiences could be very large even when the place where he would speak was outside the towns and the speaking conditions were far from ideal.

It would be wrong, however, to assume that these famous "speeches" of Christ before massed audiences were typical of his method of communication. Most of the time he was presenting his gospel of salvation — always in that same concrete and personal Semitic style — to smaller groups of people. In fact, it would seem that Christ did not ordinarily look for large crowds. They, instead, simply came to him after hearing of his reputation as a wonder-worker and controversial young rabbi. When they came, without previous instruction in his message, he would speak to them — but the New Testament indicates that Christ was far more ready to get away from large audiences than to seek them out.

How then did Christ preach? We know that he taught through examples and parables and "without parables he did not teach them." It is important to keep in mind that many of these parables were told around a supper table or during a walk through the fields or along the lake. Christ "preached" among a group of friends in the comfortable home of Martha, Mary, and Lazarus at Bethany, in the dusty road before the gate of Jericho, while walking in the evening with Nicodemus, or while sitting by Jacob's well near the town of Sichem. The gospel was "proclaimed" not so much through oratory, even Semitic oratory, as through discussion, questions, answers, homely examples, and friendly conversation.

The mystery of the kingdom of God was not presented in an ordered and logical way in the preaching of Christ, with the deductions of the philosopher or the relentless drive of the lawyer, the precision of the engineer or the clarity of the mathematician. The clarity of the gospel was the clarity of the poet; the words of Christ were the warm and colorful words of the artist. There were, of course, strong words as well as gentle words; and they were often full of a special urgency and forcefulness, but they respected the freedom of the listeners. Contention, debate, dialectic, philosophic inquiry — these were the weapons of his enemies. Christ was silent before Herod, who longed for argument. And it was Pilate who indulged in abstract speculation when he asked "What is truth?" The question was, of course, a legitimate one; but for Christ the answer was much too precious for a debater's game.

Christ wanted to reveal something of the mystery of his Father, and he chose the language of poetry rather than the language of abstraction as the best means of doing this. He ignored the prevalent Graeco-Roman rhetoric in favor of the stories, parables, and symbols of the Old Testament tradition. He was inductive and concrete in the Oriental fashion. In the same way, he preferred the discussion, the conversation, the dialogue to the oration or lecture. Christ, the great teacher, clearly favored the small seminar in an intimate setting over the lecture method in an *aula magna.*

Our difficulty is, of course, that "proclaiming the good news" has taken on a restrictive meaning which it did not have in the New Testament. "Preaching" has come to mean a sort of sacred oration or lecture, a monologue from a rather clear and structured text, given customarily before a silent audience. But for Christ and the men of the New Testament who were active "in the ministry of the Word" (Acts 6:4), this would have been far too narrow a concept.

The preaching of Christ and of his disciples, then, was wider and more encompassing than the "pulpit preaching" of later times. The "proclamation of the good news" was such a rich and expansive concept that it could not be limited in rhetoric nor in manner of presentation. Nevertheless, even in the New Testament, preaching assumed certain general forms that varied according to whom the message was directed. We can recognize them today.

There are, first of all, the people who have not yet heard the gospel or have heard it only in a very inadequate way. They are in need of missionary preaching that could lead them to an acceptance of the faith. This first phase of preaching is evangelization. An audience is introduced to Christ for the first time. The preaching of the good news is centered around the Lord Jesus himself; the story of Christ is told from Old Testament prophecies through the resurrection and the promise of his return. As Domenico Grasso says:

> The most important place among the facts of salvation history is occupied by the Death and Resurrection of Christ, especially by the Resurrection, which is the center of all salvation history. The presentation of Christ carried out in evangelization is not so much theological or apologetic as kerygmatic. The Apostles are so full of Christ, so transported by their contact with Him, that they seek their listeners' adherence to Christ through sheer, contagious enthusiasm. Christ is the Lord to whom we must give ourselves, because he has loved us first and loved us unto death.[1]

The purpose of this first type of preaching is the conversion of the listeners, a general and overall acceptance of the person of Christ as their Savior. Greater detail about who Christ is and what his salvation means will come only later. At this point, the hearer accepts the word of God with gladness and makes a total dedication of himself to God, turning away from whatever would prevent his moving toward this happiness that has now been announced to him.

Evangelization is a preaching of the "core message" which, of course, can be announced in different ways by Christ himself, Peter, Paul, Augustine, the missioners in pagan lands, and those who preach in the big, de-Christianized cities of Europe or America. Some listeners will be better prepared than others; there will be adaptation to particular situations in Africa, in Japan, or in the United States. There has even been a great deal of interest in the important question of "preevangelization," in which the minds and hearts of the listeners might be properly prepared to hear the news of salvation with openness and joy. But always this preaching is directed to people who are, in fact, hearing about Christ effectively for the first time.

This first encounter with Christ through preaching and this first attraction to him is followed by a second phase of preaching. It is a preaching of initiation that aims to impart a knowledge of the faith in all its doctrinal and moral implications. The friendship with Christ, the dedication to God that the well-disposed listener made, must now be deepened. It is the time for instruction, for catechesis, for the formation of a Christian mentality and conscience. It must be, of course, more than the systematic exposition of Christian doctrine; it must introduce the convert to those great biblical and liturgical signs that can mold his or her whole personality.

In the early church, the whole of Lent formed a time for catechetical preaching, preparing the converts for their Easter baptism. The Apostles' Creed is one of the oldest examples of catechesis. With or without the traditional questions and answers, this type of preaching is aimed at the intellect and the heart of the convert, helping him or her know Christ better through more or less systematic instruction. It is the doctrinal initiation of the catechumens and of all of those who may have received baptism but have remained uninstructed in Christian teachings.

The third form of preaching is that of formation in Christian life; the homily is for those who are already Christian. As Grasso remarks, it is "a liturgical preaching which tries to give life to the Faith already accepted and understood."[2] The homily is preached in the liturgy and is directed to the Christian community. More than that, "the one clear function of a homily is that it must achieve the upbuilding of community, the very making of the Church."[3]

It may be said that the whole liturgy works to build community. But the preaching has a special importance:

> The homily's central importance consists in the fact that it is undisputably, and in a certain sense uniquely among the elements of the eucharistic action, Christ now. The rite, the prayers, the symbolism of food, even and in some sense especially the scripture readings, may fail to convey the reality of Christ's presence to certain worshippers. But a man of their time who lives close to their lives is able to be and say Christ to them — and they to him — as no form or sign, verbal or non-verbal, can do.[4]

The Christian, who turned to Christ in his or her conversion after the preaching of evangelization, and who slowly came to understand what that conversion meant after catechetical instruction, now enters into the mystery of the Christian life in this world with greater enthusiasm and hope because of the homily that he or she hears in the liturgy. "Homiletic preaching stimulates the will to accept harmoniously the duties assumed in baptism and outlined in depth in the catechism."[5]

All three kinds of Christian preaching, evangelization, catechesis, and homily have Christ, suffering and glorious, at their center. Elements of kerygma, those basic teachings of Christianity are expanded and explained in catechesis. The homily is sometimes forced into a missionary role and must return constantly to the "core message" of kerygmatic preaching, of evangelization and conversion, since many of the assembly may still stand in need of it. It must depend on the catechetical background of the listeners, on the ordered instruction that they received in doctrine and morality — and, in a more informal way, it also continues to teach and inform.

The primary purpose of the homily, however, is not to effect the conversion of the pagan through a suitable persuasive rhetoric which would lead to a commitment of living faith, not to instruct the ignorant catechumen, child or adult, through skillful teaching methods which would form a biblical culture, but rather it is to form a eucharistic community. In a special way, it is to effect a communion with Christ in his brothers and sisters among whom we live. The purpose of the homily is the very purpose of the Eucharist itself: communion with a Person. This Person is the Second Person of the Holy Trinity, but he is discovered and served in the "least of his brothers and sisters." Communion with Christ is achieved first of all through communion with the persons around us. The homily aims to establish such a personal bond.

Communication has come to mean the transmission of a message, a message that can be measured and divided with mathematical precision. It can be analyzed and packaged for theoretically perfect delivery; but the homily, like the poem, eludes such scientific accuracy. Its purpose is not the communication of knowledge but an understanding in depth of a Person, a "communion." While it does not exclude the moving of men and women to action, it is more concerned with allowing them to experience the presence of Christ and to create a community of love and service around him.

The homily, therefore, more than any other form of preaching, has close affinities with poetry. It is not bound to be didactic any more than poetry must always teach. To share in the vision and gospel of Christ, a preaching of meditation and poetry is as necessary as the earlier evangelization and catechetical instruction. For the Bible and for the preacher of the homily, only the language of poetry seems adequate to the mystery of love and union.

From its position in the liturgy and from the example of the great Last Supper discourse of Jesus in John's Gospel, the model for homilies both in theme and spirit, the bonds of homiletic preaching with the Eucharist should have been clear and strong. But in fact liturgical preaching has had a checkered history. At times, it would seem that the purpose and nature of the homily was forgotten.

The designs of pulpits through the ages can tell us much about the kind of sermon that was heard from those pulpits. The first centuries of Christianity produced no pulpits at all, just as they produced neither churches nor altars. Secular worship was the novelty of the New Testament. The early Christians rejected the idea of worship as something separate from secular life, and they saw no difference between the secular and the sacred. They were proud of the fact that they had no sacred building or special altars. This, of course, astonished the pagans. The Eucharist was celebrated in the homes of the faithful rather than in a church building; and the homily was probably preached near the supper table, which served as an altar, to those standing around (*circumstantes*).

After Constantine, churches were built, usually modeled after the basilica or Roman public law court, which had been specially designed for public assembly, often with a semicircular dais at one end on which the judge could be seated. This place of the judge became that of the bishop, who delivered his homily seated on the episcopal *cathedra*. When Archbishop Maximian preached in the presence of the Emperor Justinian and Empress Theodora at the consecration of San Vitale in Ravenna on April 19, 547, he probably did so from his ivory throne which was placed behind the altar table. The rough stone *cathedra* of Pope St. Gregory is still preserved in San Stefano Rotondo, and it is not difficult to picture him seated there preaching one of his famous homilies, with the people gathered quite close around the altar and the seat of the bishop of Rome.

The beautiful medieval pulpits of Pisa, Siena, and Aachen indicate that preaching was moving away from the altar and from the Eucharist. The churches were larger, the people more numerous, and so pulpits were built — sometimes works of art — in order that the preachers might be better seen and heard. But they also tended to isolate the speaker, to lift him above the people, and to take him and the words he spoke ever further away from the Eucharist. Instead of the preacher speaking from behind the altar-table or from a chair nearby, he must now walk to a different area of the church, climb steps, and stand alone in an elevated position, looking down on the rest of the Christian people. It would, perhaps, be interesting to consider the psychological changes and the different attitudes toward preaching the gospel that were caused by the building of pulpits.

The Swedish historian Yngve Briloth says of this period, "Instead of being a regularly recurring element of the Mass, the sermon increasingly was reserved for special days of penance and seasons of fasting, especially the Lenten season, when spiritual oratory flowed in rich measure, at least in the cities."[6] It was not that there was a complete lack of preaching; the Franciscans and the Dominicans, who were founded in the Middle Ages for this very purpose, put increasing emphasis on preaching and built large churches to accommodate the crowds. But as the pulpits were moved further and further down the nave of the church and away from the altar, the diocesan clergy, both priests and bishops, seem to have preached less and less. Preaching was no longer closely bound to the liturgy nor was it the task of the parish priests. The speakers who are remembered from this era are the specialists like the Franciscan John of Capistran, or the famous Dominican Savonarola.

Briloth tells us:

> The pulpit became a usual fixture even though the very early pulpits were usually movable. Pews began to be customary. The friars, however, preached in many other places besides the sanctuary. Preaching to large crowds was conducive to open-air preaching even as during later periods of revival. Special preaching crosses, often magnificently ornamented, which perhaps called back memories of preaching during the Crusades, were raised in the church-yards and in public places. A story relates how Berthold of Ratisbon (Regensburg), a great and popular Franciscan preacher in thirteenth-century Germany, found the direction of the wind with a feather and then let the people settle down on the leeward side while he spoke from an improvised pulpit.[7]

There is no doubt that much of this kind of preaching was powerful and beneficial, but its relationship to the Eucharist must have been more and more difficult to appreciate. "Situations when a sermon could be presented were manifold, but among these the parish sermon in the regular Sunday Mass began to fade into the background."[8]

Renaissance and Baroque pulpits were still higher and more ornate. In many of the Gothic churches of Europe, a Baroque pulpit was installed halfway down the church. A good example is the fantastic pulpit of Louvain with its carved wooden animals and trees, quite out of place in a much older Gothic church. It provided a new focus for the eyes and ears of the people and quite frankly competed with the altar as the center of interest. The representatives of the religious orders were given the responsibility of climbing such a pulpit and meeting the demands for strong religious emotion by violent rhetorical assaults.

Baroque churches in Austria or Italy or Spain provided theatrical settings for dramatic attacks on the current enemies of the church, with biblical texts used as weapons. "Many of the weaknesses of the medieval sermon, its fondness for anecdotes, its display of learning and rhetorical bombast, its sometimes burlesque folksiness, appear again in the sixteenth and seventeenth centuries."[9] You have only to examine the famous pulpit that stands in one of the smaller churches of Cuzco, Peru, with its vanquished heretics carved beneath the figures of loyal doctors of the church, to imagine the type of sermon that was preached there. Both Protestant and Catholic sermons were long, ornate, and frequently angry.

The neoclassic pulpits of France reflect in wood, stone, and gilt the ecclesiastical oratory that sought its standards in antiquity. The Jesuit Louis de Bourdaloue (1632–1704) ignored the emotions in his effort to appeal only to intellect and will. His words are severe, cold, and clear. The Bishop of Clermont, Jean-Baptiste Massillon (1663–1743), gave ethical sermons that won the praises of Voltaire, who placed him alongside Confucius and other ethical teachers. The Lenten series, given at court, in which he recited the duties of the king to the eight-year-old Louis XV, is far removed from the spirit of the eucharistic homily.

Eighteenth- and nineteenth-century pulpits, just as most eighteenth- and nineteenth-century sermons, are rather dull copies of what had gone before. There were, of course, some later innovations (like the hydraulic pulpit in a certain parish in Joliet, Illinois — the priest walks into it at the floor level, presses a button, and slowly rises above the heads of the congregation!), but in general the quality of sermons, estranged from the liturgy, was not improved. In fact, from the building of the Jesuit churches of the Gesù and San Ignacio in Rome, thousands of churches, both Catholic and Protestant, have been built as magnificent lecture halls for doctrinal instruction and moralistic discourse. For Catholics, there *was* still a liturgy, often very splendid, and therefore a need for the church building to serve as a theater in which to watch a distant ceremonial presented before the backdrop of a towering, golden high altar. But the bond between sermon and sacrificial banquet had been forgotten. In many cases, the ethical exhortations, the panegyrical *oraisons funèbres*, and the polemic orations that have come from pulpits since the Counter Reformation have been the work of "homiletical strategists" who rolled out citations from scripture as from an arsenal of heavy artillery, but who had little further interest in the Bible or the liturgy.

But what of the pulpit today? The design of the modern pulpit is also instructive, since it indicates a new attitude toward the sermon and its place in the church. Today's pulpit, as found in the churches built in the last few years, is usually closer to the altar, much smaller, and far less ornate. It is often nothing more than a lectern or ambo on which the gospel book may be placed. In older churches, the classic pulpit has sometimes been abandoned and the pastor speaks from a simple reading stand close to the altar. This change is partially due, of course, to the fact that the pulpit canopy is no longer needed as a sounding board to project the voice of the speaker. Then too, the altar-table itself has been moved much closer to the people and the pastor stands facing them in a new relationship. (At St. Severin in Paris, the priest stands in his place behind the altar-table to give his homily.) But the preference for a new location for the act of preaching is the result of more than the installation of microphones. It shows a new appreciation of the link between liturgy and preaching. It is really a return to the tradition of the house churches of the early centuries. The elevated pulpit is abandoned not because of the loss of respect for preaching but because of a new understanding of its relationship with the Eucharist and of the nourishment that comes in both word and sacrament.

For as St. Jerome made clear, "... we're nourished on his

flesh and... we slake our thirst with his blood, not only in the Eucharistic mystery, but also in the reading of Scripture."[10] And Bernard of Clairvaux preached on the Feast of All Saints: "He himself feeds us by his deeds and his words, and even by the flesh of his own Son, which is truly food.... Therefore, we who are about to receive, through his kindness, even the spotless sacrament of the Lord's body during the holy banquet at the altar, have to be fed now by his deeds and his words."[11]

In the Gospel according to John, in the beautiful sixth chapter, it is very difficult to tell what concerns the word alone and what concerns the Eucharist. They seem to form a common gift in which the Lord promised to remain and vivify his followers. At the Last Supper the promise was to be fulfilled.

Just as the pastor breaks the bread of the Eucharist for the people in order to nourish them, and offers them the cup to refresh their weary spirits, so too that same pastor must nourish and refresh them with the word of the Lord. Jesus shows us the way. The form of his meal that springtime night in the upper room and today in our churches is simple and humble. Yet it is attractive and easily accepted. It has substance and savor. Bread and wine, food and drink, body and blood — these gifts are rich in meaning and yet are elemental, deeply rooted in the history and the present lives of men and women. Our preaching word should have these same qualities. Like the Eucharist itself, it should be *viaticum*, food for the journey, something to nourish the Christian people on their way. Its form should also have a noble simplicity, attractive taste, and real substance for the hungry. And like the Eucharist, it should lead to an encounter and communion with Christ and our sisters and brothers, more a moment of faith and mystery than of logical communication.

Preaching, like the Eucharist, is an event of today. It is not a dead memorial, a nostalgic historical pageant, a carefully accurate reconstruction of what is finished and lifeless. Christian preachers not only bring a message, "tell the story" of Jesus, but — as witnesses — they offer testimonials to truth that provoke a response. The Last Supper account is not the mere historical record of an ancient banquet, nor are the teachings of Christ to be studied like those of Marcus Aurelius. We are not sages, teachers of a body of wisdom, historians relating our research on interesting past events. Rather, we proclaim a living Person, the risen Christ, and celebrate a present event, the salvation of this generation.

The word of God is heard *now*. An encounter takes place between Jesus and the Christian community which is gathered around this particular pulpit and altar-table. The "sacramental" and the "spoken Christ" are one. It is the Lord Jesus among his people. Somehow, we pastors and preachers are part of the mystery. Somehow, in this strange world of martyrs and microchips, nuclear warheads and TV commercials, heroism and cynicism we have been called to give Jesus our voices. Frequently we are painfully aware of our limitations; many times we wonder at God's wisdom in choosing the likes of us. We want to stop, as Origen once did in the middle of a homily, and sincerely beg our listeners: "Help me with your prayer so that I may really speak God's word to you." We tremble at the words of the *Didache* that "every prophet who teaches the truth without putting it into practice is a false prophet."[12] We pray that we may "follow a straight course in preaching the truth" (2 Tim. 2:15).

"The preacher has the awesome responsibility of speaking no word that God cannot accept as his own."[13] And so we read with care and love the scriptural passages; we strive to hear what God is saying to us today; we work to find the words that God would have us say to our communities at this time. "The one who speaks is to deliver God's message" (1 Pet. 4:11). At last we must be able to say with Paul, in all humility and truth, "Christ...speaks in me" (2 Cor. 13:3).

We sense the dangers of our vocation, but we also know the joy. Our fearfulness has brought us to prayer; our ignorance has led us back to the biblical text; our weakness has forced us to depend on the Lord, and we know he has done great things for us. It is his kindness that allows us "to preach as Jesus did" and his grace that lets us say:

> Something which has existed since the beginning
> that we have heard,
> and that we have seen with our own eyes;
> that we have watched
> and touched with our hands:
> the Word, who is life — this is our subject.
>
> (1 John 1:1)

• 6 •

SAVORING THE TEXT

Behind every lector and preacher is their piety. And behind the piety and preaching of every age is the Bible, constant source and inspiration. But the way this Bible is read is, in turn, inevitably conditioned by the technology of the period. As Christians of the age of technology, it is both disturbing and fascinating for us to explore how communion through the word is aided or hindered by the way we read our Bible.

Perhaps it is time to recognize the influence of both Gutenberg and Marconi on our religious life, our personal and community prayers, and our proclamation of the word.

It is quite possible, however, that we are much closer, in our approach to God and life, to a Christian from the year 1100 than to one from the year 1800 — or even from 1900.

> We are today as far into the electric age as the Elizabethans had advanced into the typographical and mechanical age. And we are experiencing the same confusions and indecisions which they had felt when living simultaneously in two contrasted forms of society and experience. Whereas the Elizabethans were poised between medieval corporate experience and modern individualism, we reverse their pattern by confronting an electric technology which would seem to render individualism obsolete and corporate interdependence mandatory.[1]

We can only try to imagine what it meant to be a pre-Gutenberg person living in a world that, though it was not without books, had so few that they were carefully preserved by the universities or in the libraries of great abbeys or convents. A castle might have a small collection of religious or secular works, but the parish priest had to be satisfied with his office book and Missal and one or two lives of the saints. Of the books that were available, no two were exactly alike since they probably came from the hands of different scribes. The very quality of the manuscript page was different from that of a printed book. The lettering itself was given plastic stress to an almost sculptural degree. The letters had an iconic and monumental form and they were not read in a rapid and easy manner. There was a great deal of abbreviation; punctuation was not clear; the words tended to run together. Clearly, any thought of "speed reading" was unknown. In fact, it is very doubtful that silent reading existed at all. Reading was not a casual thing but a task that required one's complete attention and involved much more than eyes scanning a page. St. Benedict found it necessary to order his monks not to disturb others in doing their spiritual reading. Each word was vocalized and "tasted" by the reader. There had been no divorce between the eye and speech in the act of reading and none was contemplated.

If we, as modern Americans, tend to associate the movement of the lips and a muttering of the words with poor reading, it is because of a merely visual approach in our education. Gerard Manley Hopkins was much closer to medieval practice and spirit when he wrote:

> Of this long sonnet above all remember what applies to all my verse, that it is, as living art should be, made for performance and that its performance is not reading with the eye but loud, leisurely, poetical, (not rhetorical) recitation, with long rests, long dwells on the rhyme and other marked syllables, and so on. This sonnet should be sung: it is most carefully timed in tempo rubato.[2]

The manuscript page, with its lack of punctuation and other visual aids, demanded oral reading, a tactile stress in word use, and a vigorous involvement in the text which is not required by the uniformity and clarity of the printed line. But when we are faced with a page of Gertrude Stein, of e. e. cummings, or

Pound, or Eliot, we also find ourselves forced to do just what the medieval reader had to do. When punctuation is absent, or is not full and systematic, we return to reading aloud. We become participants in a full and involved oral action.

The medieval man considered reading as an exercise in which lips, tongue, face — we may really say his whole body — took an active part. While the lips were carefully pronouncing the words, the ears were listening to those words, the mind was stimulated, and the heart was moved. In speaking of the meaning of the *lectio divina* for St. Benedict and his monks, Dom Jean Leclercq says:

> When *legere* and *lectio* are used without further explanation, they mean an activity which, like chant and writing, requires the participation of the whole body and the whole mind. Doctors of ancient times used to recommend reading to their patients as a physical exercise on an equal level with walking, running or ball-playing.[3]

Leclercq points out the way this type of reading influenced the whole conception of prayer and meditation for the pre-Gutenberg Christian:

> This results in more than a visual memory of the written words. What results is a muscular memory of the words pronounced and an aural memory of the words heard. The *meditatio* consists in applying oneself with attention to this exercise in total memorization; it is, therefore, inseparable from the *lectio*. It is what inscribes, so to speak, the sacred text in the body and in the soul. This repeated mastication of the divine words is sometimes described by use of the theme of spiritual nutrition. In this case the vocabulary is borrowed from eating, from digestion, and from the particular form of digestion belonging to ruminants. For this reason, reading and meditation are sometimes described by the very expressive word *ruminatio*. For example in praising a monk who prayed constantly, Peter the Venerable cried: "Without resting, his mouth ruminated the sacred words." Of John of Gorze it was claimed that the murmur of his lips pronouncing the Psalms resembled the buzzing

of a bee. To meditate is to attach oneself closely to the sentence being recited and weigh all its words in order to sound the depths of their full meaning. It means assimilating the content of a text by means of a kind of mastication which releases its full flavor. It means, as St. Augustine, St. Gregory, John of Fecamp and others say in an untranslatable expression, to taste it with the *palatum cordis* or in *ore cordis*. All this activity is, necessarily, a prayer; the *lectio divina* is a prayerful reading. Thus, the Cistercian, Arnoul of Boheriss, will give this advice: "When he reads, let him seek for savor, not science. The Holy Scripture is the well of Jacob from which the waters are drawn which will be poured out later in prayer. Thus there will be no need to go to the oratory to begin to pray; but in reading itself, means will be found for prayer and contemplation."[4]

It is small wonder, then, that the early and classic texts of the spiritual life, such as the *Rule of St. Benedict*, say only a little about prayer and speak about it so unsystematically. But the *Rule* does speak about the *lectio divina* and it was in this reading that the riches of the Bible and the liturgy could be assimilated and could nourish the interior life of the individual.

Louis Bouyer, in his *Introduction to Spirituality*, mentions various methods of reading. There was, first of all, the *lectio continua* which was a complete reading of the whole Bible. Each book of the Bible was read as a whole and the whole Bible was read each year. The reader immersed himself in the world of the Bible and became absorbed in it. The continuous reading, done necessarily by fragments, would be supplemented by a reading, now and then, of one or another book of the Bible as a whole book, since each book has its own personality. It is good to discover a book of the Bible as a unit and a living whole. This reading would be guided by liturgical tradition and would follow the phases of the liturgical year. There is also the *lectio divina* properly so called, the prime concern of the reflections and counsels of ancient spiritual literature and the basic food of all spirituality. The text would usually be from sacred scripture, but it could also come from the liturgy of the church or be some other great text from religious tradition. But it is essential that it be a clear echo of scripture and lead the reader back to it.

Father Bouyer tells the modern reader who would attempt the *lectio divina:*

> This text should preferably be brief as compared with the length of time we are to devote to it. The idea is not to launch into a swift voyage of discovery, but to trace and retrace our path, to explore thoroughly, to make truly our own some part of the country hitherto known but superficially and assimilated imperfectly. Normally, we would choose a text contained in the *lectio continua* for this season of the liturgical year. Or else we could take a text more or less directly connected with the season, so as to have the benefit of all the atmosphere, the environment which the liturgical life provides for our meditation.[5]

But he realizes that such an approach is not an easy one for the post-Gutenberg man whose reading has been shaped by print technology with its uniformity and the absolute dominance of the visual, its emphasis on speed and the gathering of information, and the separation of intellectual content and feeling. He warns:

> The idea here is that of reading in order to read — not what we usually do: read in order to have read. Our greatest difficulty, perhaps, in trying to appreciate and to practice *lectio divina* as the ancients did is that we are spoiled with regard to reading, any reading. For them, books were a rarity. It was a great thing to have a book at one's disposal, and one made the most of it like a miser, or, better, like a gourmet who slowly savors his small portion so as not to lose the least crumb of it. Again, papyrus or parchment was expensive. Space, then, was not to be wasted, the words followed one another with no space in between; to read a text like this was a task in itself. This is why, as we see in the Acts, the eunuch from Ethiopia, reading the book of Isaias while riding in his chariot, was overheard by the deacon Philip as he walked along the road — people always read at least *sotto voce.* The proper sense of the Latin *meditari,* from which our word "meditate" is derived, is precisely this vocal rumination — obviously much better adapted to

the purpose of impregnating us with what we read than is
our kind of reading, the mere rapid running of the eyes
across the printed page.[6]

This kind of reading requires a special quality of attentive-
ness, a concentration of all of man's faculties on the word that
is before us. As Bouyer insists:

> The Word we read is not made to remain in the head, but
> to descend into the heart — taking the word "heart," of
> course, in the biblical sense: not as the source of the emo-
> tions only, but as the core or focus of the whole personality
> at its deepest, that intimate sanctuary in which our eternity
> is at stake because here is where our ultimate decisions are
> woven and taken.
>
> It is in this spirit, then, that we must assimilate each
> word, each thought of the text, going over them unceasingly
> until they open out and the current of the Spirit Who chose
> them flows freely into us. "Te totum applica ad textum, rem
> totam applica ad te," as the exegete Bengel said: "Apply
> yourself wholly to the text, and apply its matter wholly to
> yourself."[7]

But the question we find ourselves asking is if such a reading
of scripture is possible today? Typography has permeated every
phase of the arts and sciences for the last five hundred years.
The principles of continuity, uniformity, and repeatability have
become the basis of production, entertainment, and science. We
have lived with the idea of time and space as continuous measurable quantities. Both the world of nature and the world of
power have been secularized. Physical processes have been controlled by techniques of segmentation and fragmentation; God
and nature were separated. But, above all, the development of
printing, mechanical standardization, and specialism has separated the roles of knowledge and the roles of action. In such a
world, is it truly possible to return to an authentic *lectio divina*
and to the biblical spirituality that it would surely foster?

It would seem that "things began to change in the Byzantine
Orient when the liturgical office became complicated and over-
weighted. In the West, the crisis became even more acute from

the moment that the liturgical language ceased to be understood by the mass of Christians."[8] Piety became, in the lives of many, a series of devout practices and prayers with little interaction. And at the end of the Middle Ages, mental prayer and vocal prayer came to be considered two independent and secretly opposed realities. There was a celebration of public prayer from the time of the apostles, but with the development of monasticism this community prayer became much more complex, and its very richness and amplitude made it difficult for the Christian laity to take part. Even the clergy began to find this long public celebration burdensome, and both laity and clergy began to seek private prayers and devotions to take the place of the Divine Office and even of the Mass since these public prayers were no longer meaningful. Of course, the clergy continued to say the Breviary in private and to offer the Mass, but more and more it was a "private Mass" or a "Mass of devotion" and not a celebration of priest and people. The word of God was not heard in the liturgy and even at a "public" Mass the people merely watched a sort of sacred pageant in which certain gestures or movements of the ministers were to remind them of events in the passion of Christ. The liturgy had become an ornate court ceremonial to rival that of an earthly ruler. The time when the whole community, in the ancient church, had devoted a part of each Saturday night to prepare, by a "Service of the Word," for the Sunday eucharistic celebration was long past. At best, they had come to be only silent spectators watching something beautiful and mysterious and listening to a choir singing in a language they could not understand.

And yet the man of the Middle Ages could still be considered a "man of the Bible." Although he was cut off from the Bible in the liturgy, he lived in a world in which there was still a strong and resonant echo of the sacred scriptures. Sermons, such as those of St. Bernard, were based on the Bible and often contained its warmth and vigor. The art of the Romanesque and the Gothic churches and cathedrals, the stone of Le Puy and Autun and the stained glass of Chartres and Aachen, the tiny paintings in the numerous Books of Hours, and the mystery and morality plays — all were expressive of the Bible and its spirit. Although the medieval man had his problems and his superstitions, he was not ignorant of at least the basic outlines of salvation history. Chaucer's pilgrims feel "at home" with the Bible; biblical images and quotations came easily to people's lips. But what is still more important, most of the biblical mentality was still theirs. The split between sense and sensibility, between the rational and the affective, between God and nature, had not yet taken place.

By the sixteenth century in most of Europe this biblical approach to life had certainly disappeared. Life had become fragmented and self-conscious. Medieval man in his feudal and tribal society lived a "family" life, centered in his community. (The monastery was the very type and perfect expression of this "closed society," an extension of the family with a "Father" abbot and monks who are "brothers," each with his own role and responsibilities for the common good.) The man of the Renaissance, however, was an individual, aware of his psychology and individual importance, but with the seeds of alienation already planted in his heart. His society was open and impersonal; his loyalties were national rather than local; he was independent but also isolated since he had lost a sense of community.

Bouyer admits that "the world, in which everything human took on a new luster, was a world impassioned but also secretly anguished. It is not a very good sign when the overdevelopment of the intelligence tends toward the purely cerebral, nor does the sensibility coming to reinforce it improve matters when it turns to aggravating the emotions."[9]

St. Teresa, St. Ignatius, and those who came after them found themselves in an atmosphere created by a new technology, an atmosphere in which the psychology of the Bible had become strange and its literary style alien. If one is to understand a book, it is necessary not only to know the language in which it is written, but also to have a sympathetic feeling for the mental makeup of the culture to which the author belonged. It was, in fact, almost impossible for the men and women of the last four or five hundred years to have such a sympathetic feeling for the Semitic oral style which is found in the books of the Bible. The modern mind is more at home with the hard facts of geometry and physics than with the imponderable subtlety that scripture demands.

To return to the word of God as the center of the spiritual life means much more than a regular reading of the sacred text in the way we would read a periodical or a textbook. It means an understanding of the Semitic mentality and its oral style, and — let us admit — even a return to such a mentality and style. As Dom Celestin Charlier indicates, "The sapiential frame of mind reflected by the Bible is far from being the prerogative of the Semite. In some ways it is more characteristic of the Far East, the Chinese and Hindus for example, and of the Slav peoples. It is not unknown in the West, as the present vogue of existentialist philosophies bears witness."[10] According to the center of reference men have taken, they move toward the technical side of human thought or the moral and sapiential side, toward the clarity and precision of the "fixed point of view" and the printed page or the symbolism, mysticism, even obscurity found in the oral and manuscript culture. Perhaps it is overly simple to call one trend "Greek" and the other "Semitic," and it would be better to speak of "Eastern" and "Western" mentalities or "ancient" and "modern" approaches. But the clearest division would seem to be between the man of the "closed" society, dependent on and integrated into his community or tribe and the independent man of the "open" society — literate, separate, detached from the world in which he lives; between the man of audial-tactile culture and the man of isolated visual culture.

As Charlier remarks:

> People who cannot think except in the logic of Aristotle or Descartes are disconcerted by what they call the "incoherence" and "obscurity" of the Bible. If they are critics or philologists, they tend to see every break in logic as a sign that the text has been tampered with, or a new source introduced. If they are philosophers or moralists, they harp on the Semitic inability to be abstract or speculative, and welcome the advent of the Greek mind which was able to put some precision into this childish babbling.[11]

This radical difference between the Eastern and Western dialectic is not only the breeding ground for a great deal of misunderstanding of the Bible's true character; it is also the cause of a distrust of biblical spirituality and a lack of ease with the Bible and the liturgy. Dom Celestin Charlier sees the problem in this way:

The Greek (and the rest of the western world after him) used his mind and his words to express ideas, as succinctly as possible. He believes that such expression is possible because he uses as his starting point the world of external reality, which itself is distinct and measurable. The Semite, on the other hand, does not separate himself from the world in which he lives. He is not detached, he does not stand outside that world, he is part of it. His starting point is within himself, his own personal experience, which he cannot contain in words because words have no place there. He does not attempt to "express" what is in his mind, he simply tries to "evoke" it.

The Greek reconstructs and re-creates the outside world within the framework of his mind. The Semite takes what is already in his mind and tries to transmit it by suggestion. The Greek abstracts and arrives at a universal idea; the Semite fastens on to the particular and tries to absorb it. The Greek is concerned to conceive truth and demonstrate it; the Semite seeks to receive it and make other people want it. Conceiving and receiving, active and passive, these are the words which best sum up the two attitudes.[12]

The different dialectics have their own types of logic. The perfection of the syllogism characterizes the Greek dialectic. Points must be dealt with in order, and a new idea must wait until the first idea has been fully treated. The science of mathematics is applied to the field of the mind. It is felt that what can be clearly conceived can be clearly expressed, and the result is a masterly Greek, or Latin, or English "period" in rhetoric.

But the Eastern dialectic rejects demonstration of thought. It must not compel the mind but rather try to give it a feeling for life and reality. It does not sense the diversity of things, but their unity.

To abstract is to weaken and amputate and eventually to kill. In its place the Semite builds up a concept by superimposing one suggestion on another. His thought does not proceed in a straight line but in concentric circles, where one affirmation is the repetition or antithesis of the one before. The Semite states what he has to say, and then several more times, adding each time another touch, another stroke, constantly enriching this or that aspect of a thought which was already present in its entirety in the first formulation.[13]

For such an Eastern mentality, poetry may be considered the "normal" mode of expression. The Semite feels relaxed and freed from restraint in poetry, while the Western man, who may well move from prose to poetry, feels that he must put on "formal dress" to do so.

The Greek mind found its perfect expression in the printed line of Gutenberg technology. It delighted in lineal movement, uninvolved and visual. But this is far from the ear and drum technology of tribal man, the world of hearing and speaking and touching in which the Semite lives and moves. And this latter is the world of the Bible.

Henri Daniel-Rops looks at the Bible and says:

Who thinks, as he thumbs the closely printed pages, of the time when these words and sentences were not fixed in cold print but chanted or intoned to audiences by the voices of the Heralds of God?

Long before it was a written text, by far the greater part of the Bible was oral teaching. In the form of more or less stereotyped narratives, rhythmic and assonant poems, and pithy proverbs and sayings, its elements were handed down from generation to generation by the spoken word before the use of writing became general. This rather special kind of genesis, of which other oriental books (the Koran, for example) provide examples, is intimately related to the cultural, spiritual and linguistic patterns of the people among which the Bible grew up, patterns of simple and communal type in which literary creation was much less individual and intellectual, and more living and spontaneous, than among us....

Transmission by memory and the spoken word was greatly facilitated by the technique applied to it. There was an art of learning by heart that formed part of the art of composition. This oral style has left a visible mark on the text; the written version to a large extent preserves its patterns. The regularity of the rhythm, the repetition of certain words and the use of alliteration assisted the memory. We have only to read aloud many passages in the Gospels to become aware of the oral phrasing behind the written text.[14]

It is really not strange that the oral process was about the same for the New Testament as for the Old Testament. The Gospels were first "spoken" and later written down, probably from notes, to make the apostolic teaching more permanent. The Acts of the Apostles and the Apocalypse were written documents and were presented as such, but the Epistles of St. Paul were "dictated" and in them the oral style appears again. And these letters were, for the most part, intended for oral communication in the various Christian communities.

What are the characteristics of this "oral style"? They are few and simple. "Parallelism" is the very hallmark of both Semitic poetry and prose; it is used to give precision to the primary statement and build up a gradual and insistent rhythm. It causes the same idea to be presented again and again, but always with a slightly different facet. The repetitions ebb and flow with a force that makes them easy to remember and allows the basic idea to sink into the heart. The Beatitudes give us a good example from the New Testament.

The Semite refuses to analyze and so his syntax is based on coordinate rather than subordinate clauses. But the conjunctions that link so many phrases together are themselves lacking in logical precision, and so the juxtaposition, which is such a common characteristic of the Eastern style, often gives a richness and a subtle variety of meanings. The position of the phrases may be either artful or spontaneous, but they help us in an intuitive way to understand the desired shade of meaning.

Since the Semite is delighted by a paradox and since he enjoys contrasting reality with nonreality, he is given to using antithesis. He will state a theme, quickly give its opposite, and often leave his listener to form his own synthesis.

He is suspicious of the abstract and, therefore, he makes great use of symbolism. But even his symbolism is not that of the Western world. "For the Greek, the symbol is a signpost which points to an abstract idea, a mere convention which enables the writer to express his thought. For the Semite it is something more. One could almost say that for him the whole of reality, of thought and of life is a symbol."[15]

This world he sees as a reflection of the invisible world, and he wants the words that he uses to talk about it to embody something of the reality of the world, to suggest the concrete and the living. He will use a parable, but he does not want to split it up into its constituent elements in the manner of a Greek allegory. We are not to draw logical and systematic conclusions from it; we must respect the mystery that it represents.

The Semite enjoys great freedom of style; he is really not concerned about the manner of his expression as long as the inspiration and movement in his soul are given to his listeners. The elements of his style are those of the man who speaks rather than writes, and they flow naturally from the energy and rhythm of thought and the spoken word.

In our highly literate society with its very self-conscious literary intelligentsia, it is hard to realize the spontaneous quality of this literature with its rambling logic but with its rhythm and compulsion. The authors pay far more attention to their inspiration than to their style. They are not rationalists but men of passion and warm conviction. They speak from the "heart," which for a Semite is not the mere seat of his affections but the very center of his life and thought.

> There is no point in looking for metre and stanza and rules for versifying, since these things do not strictly speaking exist. The only thing that exists is the pulsing rhythm of the poet's own overflowing soul, and the transmission of the vibrant waves, that radiate from his intuitive genius.[16]

However, is it possible that we ourselves are now more "Semitic" than we realize? Could it be, as Marshall McLuhan some years ago suggested, that we are at last entering a new era, the age of electric technology where communication no longer depends on the printed line but on the spoken voice and moving pictures seen simultaneously in all parts of the world, the age of the computer in which specialism, the fragmentation of knowledge, has become obsolete, the age in which nationalism becomes meaningless, the split of man into a public and private self becomes foolish, and the interdependence of all becomes clear and real? In other words, are we at the opportune moment to enter again into the world of the Bible?

Only a short time ago such a return would have been impossible. Charles Moeller indicates how far Hebraic thought is from the divided man of the last few centuries:

> The psychology and, consequently, the anthropology of the Old Testament ignore all dualism: the word "flesh" (*basar*) does not mean the body (for which there is no word in Hebrew), but the whole created being ("body and soul," if we are thinking of man as envisaged by our Hellenistic way of thinking) in his basic weakness, both ontological and moral, before the living God: the word "spirit" then, does not mean primarily something which is discarnate, but life in its aspect of power, which exists supremely in the living God, the Lord of "spirits" and of all "flesh."[17]

This unified vision of man and of life, both so ancient and so in keeping with today's mentality, conditioned by instant electric technology rather than by a mechanical and lineal one, helps explain biblical literary style:

> And, finally, certain peculiarities of Hebraic style — parallelism, the parable genre, accounts which seem to make the role of secondary causes evaporate into thin air, a language that is concrete and dynamic (every Hebrew verb expresses a movement, and act); the "word" (*dabar*) is a reality, a creative force.... [18]

Hans Urs von Balthasar is certainly hopeful when he says,

> Perhaps we can understand the mystery of Israel better than could any Christian age in the past, better even than the apostolic age itself in its context of Judaism and Hellenism.... The more the concrete and historical human element is precisely defined, the more the revealed truth is seen to be profound, the more it stands out clearly; this is one of the great laws opposed to gnosticism, a law of the incarnation.... Time is in no way a uniform stream; it

knows mysterious moments of concentration, climaxes in
which man frees himself and chooses himself; he is, at the
same time, in the tradition of the Bible and in the spirit of
Einstein.[19]

New concepts of space and time sound strangely like biblical
concepts. Moeller says:

One theme that dominates both the Biblical and liturgical
movement is that expressed in the word today, *hodie.* The
man of the Bible is of today; he is always of the present
time, he is always close to us, because he is always close
to God, creating according to God, and the today of the
Bible opens on eternity. It is enough to penetrate into the
soul of a twentieth-century man in order to cause that deep
water to spring forth from which will be reborn, recreated
by grace, the man of the Bible.... [20]

Perhaps it is an age of electric circuits, television, and telephone that will again appreciate the living word and its liturgical
celebration in a community, and rediscover the pattern of the
early church.

Giving the first complete description of the liturgical assembly of the faithful, St. Justin in the second century writes in his
First Apology:

On the day which is called Sunday we have a common
assembly of all who live in the cities or in the outlying dis-
tricts, and the memoirs of the Apostles or the writings of
the Prophets are read, as long as there is time. Then, when
the reader has finished, the president of the assembly ver-
bally admonishes and invites all to imitate such examples
of virtue. Then we all stand up together and offer up our
prayers, and as we said before, after we finish our prayers,
bread and wine and water are presented.[21]

Here is the pattern: biblical reading — explanation — eucharistic sacrifice. At Troas, St. Paul gave his discourse when
the Christians had gathered together on a Sunday evening, and
then there was the "breaking of bread," and the eating of it (Acts

20:7–20). And Christ himself at the Last Supper established the very type of the principal liturgical function when he united his holy teaching, words of comfort, exhortation, and prayer with the institution of the Eucharist, the sacrificial action. As Cardinal Bea well said:

> The singular efficacy inherent in the word of God by virtue of its own nature is increased and given new power, as it were, by its union with the eucharistic Sacrifice. The assembly of the faithful who come together to assist at the celebration of the eucharistic Sacrifice is in reality the most propitious setting for the fruitful reading and explanation of the word of God.... Here this reading of the sacred Books is surrounded with the mysterious recollection found in the house of God and the reverent ceremonies with which the Church honors the sacred Book. Here is found that sense of spiritual community which unites the faithful of a parish with one another and with their pastor. Here the attention and devotion of some worshipers transmits itself almost spontaneously to the rest, and there is created an atmosphere of spiritual receptiveness, interior preparation which is hard to come by in another environment.[22]

It is this union of word and Eucharist that the church recognizes as the center of her liturgy. It is in this union that preaching has been developed and found a home, suffering a loss of vitality whenever it has been separated from it. And it is in this union of word and Eucharist that Christians today are again finding a worthy source and integrating focus for their piety. Here too is the great religious expression for their growing sense of community and interdependence. The Gutenberg world is fading as a new electric and atomic galaxy appears. In many ways, it seems a providential development for our Christian life.

· 7 ·

A TOUCH OF THE POET

"The artist is the man in any field, scientific or humanistic, who grasps the implications of his actions and of new knowledge in his own time."[1] Is it true then that the preacher should be an artist? "The artist picks up the message of cultural and techno-logical challenge decades before its transforming impact occurs. He, then, builds models or Noah's arks for facing the change at hand."[2] Could the sermon therefore be considered such a nec-essary Noah's ark, constructed from the Bible and modern life by the artist-preacher to help the Christian community face the changes at hand?

The word of God must be spoken; it is a commission and an obligation. It would, however, be advantageous if there were people around to hear, people with ears open and hearts and minds ready for the message. If the artist must move from the ivory tower in order to prevent undue wreckage in society through technological changes, sudden and unprepared for, then the preacher must move from the ivory tower of the traditional pulpit in order to build up a Christian community which must live in that same society of change and confusion.

The preacher, therefore, must be an artist who knows and accepts the earmarks of all great art: "skepticism, contempla-tiveness, and austerity, compassion for humanity, ecstatic vision, forebodings of disaster, search for pure and significant form."[3] In any case, we are coming to realize that the sermon either shares in these qualities or it quickly becomes "kitsch" — "a kind of pseudo-art based on sentimentalized or stereotyped feeling, ad-dressed to the lowest standard of taste."[4]

70

If a Christian community today often appears somewhat bland, of a spineless and unquestioning character, without discrimination and discernment, and much given to escapism, perhaps it is because for a long, long time its sermons, its church buildings and decorations, its music — all have been varieties of "kitsch."

The sermon, therefore, must be art. The preacher must be a poet, a "maker," an "artist." Preaching must be — like art itself — "the revealing experience." And since it is no longer true that the art of one age grows directly and exclusively from the art of the previous period, as for example the art of the Gothic period grew from the forms and materials of the Romanesque, the artist of today must be open to many sources. Through research and the work of translators, the new poet may be as aware of Japanese or medieval Latin poetry as he is of Keats or Tennyson. Through the musicologist and the tape recorder, music of all periods and all places becomes available for everyone. Color reproductions make the whole history of art, from ancient Persia or modern Paris, a possible source of inspiration. The artist, faced with such richness, must of necessity be eclectic.

Nor is the preacher immune from such an embarrassment of riches, for he lives at a time of profuse biblical and theological studies that parallel the secular knowledge explosion. His own environment, like that of his listeners, is shaped by technology, by design, by the artists. Never was the irony of Oscar Wilde that life imitates art so close to the truth.

In fact, new synthetic materials and applications of energy have already brought some strange and wonderful new ways of manipulating space, sound, structure, movement, and light. The electronic amplification systems that are now installed in almost every parish church of any size not only allow large congregations to hear the preacher but also change the very shape of the sermon, just as the limitless electronic amplification of the guitar and organ has given us a new popular music.

Not too many years ago a Chicago priest suffered permanent vocal damage because he had to preach regularly in a very large church without an amplification system. The pastor of this parish, a preacher of the old school with powerful diaphragm and mighty projection, considered such amplification an unnecessary and expensive innovation, not to be tolerated. Since the death of that pastor and the installation of the loudspeakers he so dreaded, the people in the back pews can now hear the sermons. But more than that, the technology of the amplification system has created a new *kind* of sermon in that parish, a sermon which is far more conversational and intimate, far less flamboyant and intense.

The big phrase and the lush sentiment are frankly foolish when spoken into a microphone and amplified through multiple loudspeakers. But when declaimed in ringing tones by the unaided voice in a huge church, they give some of the fullness and power that Greek drama achieved with its splendidly clad actors chanting out monumental lines to an enormous audience. In both cases, large numbers of people had to be reached and moved. The style had to be larger than life.

All of this changes when the slightest whisper will be heard in every corner of a vast cathedral if it is properly amplified by electronic means. While we may doubt that the "medium is the message," it is clear that the medium determines the shape of the message. Baroque preaching has been killed by the loudspeaker. The tiny but highly sensitive microphone produces a highly sensitive and discriminating audience. Does the emergence of this more sophisticated congregation signal the doom of the preacher playing on our religious, sentimental, or political emotions?

Preaching moves to a lower key; it becomes less insistent and strident. Since "speech is a cool medium of low definition, because so little is given and so much has to be filled in by the listener,"[5] this would seem to be more in keeping with its nature. And, like other cool media such as the telephone and television, it invites audience participation. It asks that the listeners "fill in the blanks."

Unlike the printed book, which allows the silent reader to be aloof and disinterested, the cool medium of speech leads to wholeness, depth of awareness, and empathy. It is eager to have people declare themselves totally. It certainly tends to reveal the speaker, but it also tends to involve and reveal the listeners, though they may try, even desperately, to keep on their inscrutable masks.

Far more than the printed page, it moves toward an instant sensory awareness of the whole. The spoken word is quick and implicit. Should we still ask, therefore, what a sermon is about?

It is probably more valuable to ask what is the configuration of the sermon, what is its pattern?

It would seem to be already true that we want to know what a sermon achieved rather than what a sermon was about. "Concern with effect rather than meaning is a basic change of our electric time, for effect involves the total situation, and not a single level of information movement."[6] The test, therefore, is not to discover how much the listeners remember after the sermon, but how did it have its effect. The art of the sermon today, like the other arts, has become unhappy about being forced to submit to the logical knife that tries to cut apart matter and form.

Art is spoken of today as an extension of human awareness, a translator of experience. Preaching is an extension of our social selves and one of the media of communication. It is an art when it extends experience for the congregation. In the service of Christ and in obedience to him, preaching is a religious act. In the service of men and women and as a means of greater awareness and deeper experience, it is both a religious act and an artistic act that leads to communion.

Few would deny that preaching is a creative act which has, on occasion, produced works of lasting value. The literary person delights in the style of Newman in his *Plain and Parochial Sermons*. The cultured person is drawn to John Donne's sermons as well as to his poems. And every Frenchman is taught that Bossuet and Lacordaire are among the great masters of his language. But we should look not only to the literary remains of the great preachers of the past but to the very act of preaching to find the artist at work.

It may be true that the musician or poet or painter today is more concerned with the primacy of his own experience as he wrestles directly with his material. But ultimately, "his respect for his readers or audience will show through, but as an implicit or subsumed effect of his art, part of his 'good faith' as an artist. The writer or poet who consciously handles his material with the audience continually in the forefront of his mind is, often, the producer of 'mass' art: by trying to write too deliberately for his readers and his market, he ends up by writing for no one in particular."[7] This is a real danger not only for the poet but also for the preacher who sets out to "talk down to his audience" and looks for quick and easy ways of ingratiating himself with his listeners.

But it is also true that a sermon is created for the people. The preacher can never afford the luxury of a certain artistic self-indulgence, shown by some painters or poets with a cold contempt for the public. Their world is kept locked and, if the key is found, it is by accident. For certain artist-creators today, the bigger world is unwelcome. They feel no need for a comprehensive "sense of audience" since they address themselves or only a small group of *electi*.

The artist-performer, the epic poet, the troubadour, and the singer of songs have never been able to afford such isolation. Even "pop" singers must come out of hiding to go to their recording studios in Nashville or Hollywood. If these artists, together with the preacher, favor a greater interaction with their audience than others it is because, like film, television, and radio, so much depends upon the impact and immediacy of performance. Even in the traditional "high arts," the development has been away from more formal, composed, and distanced qualities and toward novelty, sensation, simultaneity, immediacy, and impact.

The very lines that traditionally divided the arts have become blurred. Film, for example, appears as a new art which is a synthesis of many arts. The line between painting and sculpture disappears in many modern works. Since the time of the Grecian odes, it has never been possible to separate perfectly the arts of song and oral interpretation. In the *Carmina Burana* of Orff or *Le Roi David* and *Jeanne d'Arc au Bucher* by Honegger, they experience a new and magnificent blending.

"In our age artists are able to mix their media diet as easily as their book diet."[8] We find T. S. Eliot making a careful use of jazz and film form. The impact of Chaplin and James Joyce is at least partially due to their blending of the lyric and the ironic. Instead of favoring conformity and routine, the new media open new relationships; they ask to be "mixed" in many shifting patterns.

At Northwestern University, a symposium was offered on "Modes and Media of Communication." It proved to be a stimulus for many experiments in blending oral interpretation with film, music, dramatic lighting, sound effects, and design. There were some heady mixtures and not everything was a success, but whole new areas were opened for further exploration. Speech (and preaching which is the more pious — but not less interesting! — of speech's rowdy children) is caught up in the innovations and excitement of the other arts. Of course there is danger that preaching might become a sort of Hollywood production, dependent on tape recorders, slides, and tricky lighting effects. Of course there is danger that the word of God could be lost among the audio-visual techniques, that the mighty God of Abraham, Isaac, and Jacob could become an excuse for a theatrical entertainment. But there is also danger that the traditional preacher, standing alone in his traditional pulpit, could become pretentious, distracting, and lost in a sense of his own importance. Indeed, it has happened more than once.

But to ignore the possibilities of the new media in the service of the word is to ignore what Edward T. Hall and other anthropologists have clearly revealed, that the spoken language is only one means of communication, that "time talks" and "space speaks," and that the people of this age receive their messages through mixed media and with a richness of sense perception — at school, in business, and in front of their color television.

This is not to say, obviously, that such richness of media is necessary or possible in our usual preaching. Many preachers do not have the time, the creative imagination, the resources, or even the energy for preaching and liturgy of this kind. Materials must be assembled, people must be trained to take part, timing must be carefully synchronized; in fact, the whole liturgy becomes a group or a parish project which brings great satisfaction and deep involvement. But all of this requires time, some money, a bit of daring, experiments, and enthusiasm. To try to do it every day, for example, could lead to exhaustion. And there have been far too many "meaningful liturgies" that have been merely silly or "cute."

But new generations appear. There are now young people who had a television set for a baby-sitter; who have never been out of earshot of a disc jockey, even while riding the subway or walking down the street; who have never ceased to hear Muzak providing background noise in stores or offices or waiting rooms; who may not have experimented with drugs but certainly have been immersed in a highly colored psychedelic culture ever since they can remember. They are different — the change is far more profound than fads in clothing or pop music.

It would be most naive to think that young men and women who have spent their whole lives swimming in sound, listening to bands whose $6,000 worth of amplification equipment can and does produce sounds so loud that some doctors claim the hearing of the young musicians will be destroyed, are any longer able to perceive the Sunday sermon in the same way. When the advertising agencies plot a commercial to hold the attention of a prekindergarten child with a magic mixture of movement, color, and sound, they are helping to create a new kind of Christian who may as an adult possibly sit in a pew but not hear the sermon, for all of the sincerity and style of the preacher. This new Christian is already among us, restless because he is not book-orientated like the preaching he hears. He does not, we may be sure, stay seated in that pew for very long; he wanders off, a church dropout for the same reason he may be a school dropout: he just does not understand the language being spoken. The preacher who speaks only Hungarian would experience difficulties giving a sermon in Tokyo. And so does the speaker of classical oratorical training when he preaches to the young fellow who is saving the money he makes at the gas station for an electric guitar, and to his girl friend, who just bought a new rock tape at Sears. Can we really say with Christ that these "poor have the gospel preached to them"?

McLuhan is right when he says that

> with electricity and automation, the technology of fragmented processes suddenly fused with the human dialogue and the need for overall consideration of human unity. Men are suddenly nomadic gatherers of knowledge, nomadic as never before, informed as never before, free from fragmentary specialism as never before — but also involved in the total social process as never before; since with electricity we extend our central nervous system globally, instantly interrelating every human experience.[9]

When McLuhan wrote those words in the sixties, he could not have dreamed that tens of thousands of Chinese young people would march for democracy in the streets of Beijing, would

be crushed by the tanks and guns of the Communist army, and
that the rest of the world would be watching it all in their living
rooms, deeply moved and outraged at such naked brutality in
1989.

What explains the constant complaint that the church is not
enough involved, that institutional religion is irrelevant, and
that our preaching does not lead to social action? Easier travel,
greater mobility, the wire services, and especially the powerful
effect of the television news-pictures and documentaries have
put pain and poverty, war and hate, prejudice and injustice in
the very center of our consciousness in a way that was impossible when we read about these things in books. Even hearing
the news on the radio or seeing a newsreel once a week after
the feature film in the local movie house did not bring the same
kind of involvement that television demands. Is it any wonder
that a preaching which does not especially concern itself with
these realities of life and death, hope and futility, which rip at
the very entrails of millions of TV viewers several times a day,
can seem effete and worthless? It becomes hard to forgive the
preacher who seems to ignore issues that sear the modern soul
when Beirut and Belfast are just beyond our city limits.

For people conditioned by books or newspapers, a presentation of views in the pulpit is quite satisfactory. But for those conditioned by technological media and involvement in depth in a
situation, an "otherworldly" sermon that has not wrestled in the
dirt of this world is unpardonable and inexplicable. Even more,
the intensely participational kind of experience has created an
audience that simply will not tolerate the aloof and authori-
tarian preacher who speaks *at* his congregation. The speaker's
credentials may be perfect, his learning enormous, his personal
piety undisputed, his sincerity manifest. He may even have great
charm and wit, style and drama. But if he does not engage his audience, if he lectures them instead of letting them "participate"
in the sermon, he is rejected by the "electric generation." For
they have grown up taking participation for granted. Involvement seems their birthright.

Unhappily, large numbers of priests and bishops and ministers, superb products of print culture, highly literate, specialists,
used to linear thinking and linear living, have not been able
to adapt to the new world where remote visualized goals are

unreal and irrelevant and where an all-inclusive "nowness" demands total involvement. They cannot understand this need for participation in areas of religion that they have long considered their private property. Their positions as religious leaders seem threatened and their reaction has been stern and unyielding. As the laity have become ever more outspoken about their rights in the church, they have been answered with still more talk about clerical and hierarchical authority.

The Pentagon, the White House, Madison Avenue, General Motors, and Hollywood are all being forced to make the difficult change from the clearly defined line of delegated authority to the more blurred — but necessary — image of the authority of knowledge and group consensus. Education, government, and business at all levels must look for new strategies of action. The church and its pulpit will have a difficult time remaining immune.

There seems little doubt fuller participation and a more diffuse kind of authority can bring much that is good. The same new preference for depth participation has prompted in the young a strong drive toward religious experience with rich liturgical overtones, and it might also be said that the ecumenical movement is synonymous with electric technology. The world becomes, more and more, a sort of global village.

When a preacher mentions the missionary work of the church, for example, those "missions" no longer seem remote and exotic. The congregation has been there, with NBC, CBS, and ABC! Some have actually visited the Holy Land, but all know of its stark landscape and bitter problems from the evening news or "Nightline." The ordination of a black woman bishop, another trip for the pope, the abortion debate on the steps of the Supreme Court, Tammy and Jimmy, medical ethics — all sorts of religious topics and personalities flash across our TV screens and our minds. Not since the days when theology caused riots in the streets of ancient Constantinople or medieval Paris have so many Christians been aware of religious issues.

Church leaders might take solace in this as they are called upon to share more of their authority and sacrifice certain dignities.

While the instantaneous global coverage of television and radio forces us out of our isolation and individualism into an almost tribal "togetherness" and a sharing of responsibilities and authority, there is panic among the pastors and preachers trained in the isolated and tightly disciplined seminaries of some years ago. Structures and traditions were revered and canonized. Nothing was seriously questioned; all things, civil and ecclesiastical, seemed stable and built for the ages.

Now, when political leaders, from prime minister to small-town mayor, must live with a daily democracy that is much more than political theory, and when the commercial sector has discovered how self-defeating is totalitarian rule for business success, there are still bishops in their dioceses, pastors in their parishes, and preachers in their pulpits who cling to privileges of a vanishing era. They fight what they feel are changes in theology and generally ignore the changes in technology that transform our way of perceiving. More tolerant listeners find them somewhat quaint and ignore them. The more choleric become frustrated and furious, denounce the defenders of the old regime — and then also ignore them. That so much formal religion and the statements of so many religious people seem irrelevant must be seen as the result of a shift in perception brought about by instantaneous communications.

Sermons are themselves mass media, since they may also be described as situations contrived to permit simultaneous participation of many people in some significant pattern of their own corporate lives. But just as the film has used the novel and television has used the film for content, the sermon has also used other media for its own purposes. We should certainly not be surprised about this exploitation or crossing of various media. The difficulty is that the sermon has used the personal essay, the scholastic disputation, or the mannered political oration as its favored forms. Unfortunately, these have not been popular or appreciated literary types for quite some time. Even these forms, now in disfavor, could receive new life through the inspired breath of an artist of some genius, just as a great musician could again write in the form of the fugue or the *concerto grosso*. In general, of course, our sermons "in the style of" Charles Lamb, a University of Paris *disputatio* (without, of course, *quaestiones ex corona*), or a Baroque or Victorian ceremonial or political oration have been stale and meager things.

The fact is that only an artist can bring the fresh and ex-

citing to any form. Only he can even keep our attention long
enough to catch our minds and hearts. There is an immediate
need for preacher-artists to keep our congregations from quietly
perishing of boredom. There have been too many "nonartists"
in our pulpits, and as McLuhan says of them, "Non-artists always look at the present through the spectacles of the preceding
age. General staffs are always magnificently prepared to fight
the previous war."[10]

Art is not a suspicious or dangerous alien to be avoided by
the preacher. Nor is it an ornamental but expendable frill in the
preparation and performance of the sermon. It is at the very
center of the preaching process and one of our chief hopes for
closing the gap between word and people in an electronic age,
for bringing us to shared experience, to awareness at a deeper
level, to compassion and "communion."

Communication, the transmission and reception of information, is an accepted function of speech and, therefore, of
preaching. Communion, on the other hand, is a less precise but
no less important concept. Communication represents a clear-
cut purpose for preaching. Communion, in its very ambiguity,
tells us something of another and more mysterious dimension.
The early alliance of preaching with classical rhetoric gave it the
benefits of clarity and force, but it also gave a rigidly persuasive
orientation, ready for argumentation and polemic, for instruction and motivation. If it looked to art, it was only to the "art"
or skill of rhetoric.

But just as a poem may establish "communion" rather than
convey "information," so too Christian preaching may quite
properly be more concerned with "communion" in one or more
of its meanings.

For the average Christian, the word "communion" often has
as its primary meaning the participation in the Lord's Supper. It
also means, of course, a sharing of ideas, of experiences, and of
feelings. It can stand for the notion of fellowship in the church,
a community of love and service in the imitation of Christ,
a union of minds and hearts around the "communion table."
It stands for that aspect of preaching which goes beyond logical discursive discourse and beyond intellectual appeals. Ultimately, communion means religion, that "binding back to God"
or union with the Divine. "Our hearts are made for you, O

God," said Augustine, "and they do not rest until they rest in you." Preaching is meant to serve this most profound and burning desire of every heart. It needs all the help that prayer and poetry can give it. For as Frederick Buechner writes:

At its heart, religion is mysticism. Moses with his flocks in Midian, Buddha under the Bo tree, Jesus up to his knees in the waters of Jordan: each of them responds to Something for which words like shalom, oneness, God even, are only pallid souvenirs. "I have seen things," Aquinas told a friend, "that make all my writings seem like straw." Religion as institution, ethics, dogma, ritual, scripture, social action — all of this comes later and in the long run maybe counts for less. Religions start, as Frost said poems do, with a lump in the throat, to put it mildly, or with the bush going up in flames.... [11]

New theologies, fresh biblical understanding, and a return to oral traditions will not allow us merely to put new wine in old wineskins. Preaching today begs for the imagination of the artist and the vision of the poet.

· 8 ·

THE EXPLOSIVE WORD

The taxi driver kept his thoughts to himself. He must have wondered, however, why a foreigner would leave central Leningrad to go to an address in the far suburbs. He left me at a large apartment complex built in the heavy style that is the ugly curse of housing projects everywhere. The smell in the lobby and the badly defaced elevator reminded me of visits to the infamous high-rise "projects" on Chicago's South Side, but when I entered the apartment of my friends, the atmosphere was pure Russian. We had not seen one another for ten years, and Sasha and Lena had invited everyone from the "old gang" plus a few new friends they knew were "safe."

Lena served us soup and roast duck, fresh cucumbers and tomatoes and — of course — lots of Russian champagne and vodka. Sasha had even managed to pick up a bottle of brandy on a Sunday! (Very resourceful, those Russians.) Ivan, a young pianist, had brought a recording he had made of the Chopin preludes, and we all listened appreciatively in the lingering twilight of summer.

Lena whispered to me, "You remember that ten years ago Pavel was an atheist. Well, he has now become a believer and he is very happy."

I looked across at Pavel and there truly seemed to be a great serenity in his eyes. With the face of a young and joyful mystic, he could have been an Alyosha who had just stepped from the pages of *The Brothers Karamazov*. But he was not the only believer there. In the course of ten years, this group of young engineers, musicians, and clerks had all become Christians. In fact, that very Sunday they had all been at the Orthodox liturgy in the Alexander Nevsky monastery or at Mass in the one Roman Catholic church that is allowed in Leningrad.

Boris went to the bookshelf as we were talking. He brought over a large and very old book which he reverently placed in my hands. Its cover was gone, the pages were yellow, and the edges frayed. But I could read the words, so subversive and dangerous, that were in large print on the top page: "The Gospel according to St. Matthew."

"This is Sasha's New Testament," Boris said, with considerable awe. "It belonged to his grandparents."

"It is very precious," Irene confided. "Sometimes one does become available on the black market, but it would cost about three hundred American dollars! It is simply impossible to buy a New Testament here. I used to go as a student to the reading room of the Kasansky Sabor on the Nevsky Prospekt, and there I could read the New Testament they kept for "atheistic research!" (The Kasansky Sabor, or cathedral of Our Lady of Kasan, is a former church that has been turned into an "anti-God" museum.)

I looked with new respect at this old and tattered book. In the United States we would have thrown it out long ago and bought a new and more legible edition. But here it was treasured as something far more than a family heirloom. It was a text that was holy and forbidden, rare and provocative, traditional and still stimulating, the glad tidings of Jesus that could not be bought at a bookshop or imported into the country. Its pages showed not only their age but also their use. Here was an antique edition of the New Testament still nourishing a new generation of Russians who had spent their lifetime in an aggressively atheistic nation.

They told me of an elderly woman they knew who was caught with a typewritten copy of a forbidden religious book. She was arrested and given only salty food and no water while she was in jail. She was finally released, but full of terror that the secret police would arrest her again, went back to her apartment and committed suicide.

Marek told the story of a highly talented young friend of his who had done very well at the university. But when he insisted that he wanted to enter the Orthodox seminary, he was taken away to a psychiatric hospital; the regime prefers a clergy who are substandard and docile.

Marek himself had been denied his doctorate in biology when the authorities discovered he was a "believer." No one who attends Christian services is ever allowed to teach, enter the professions, or be a military officer.

"Since we cannot travel abroad," said Lena, "and there is so much we cannot read, we are forced to look within ourselves and find strength in our small circle of friends, whom, of course, we must trust completely."

"Yes," Boris laughed, "if you are picked up for having forbidden literature, it is not easy to keep insisting that you found it on a park bench!"

I reverently handed back the battered New Testament. Of all the copies I have held in my life, this one seemed the most shabby — but also the most potent! None had ever seemed so like a stick of dynamite, a cause for martyrdom and yet a source of strength and celebration. Surely, it is not the dry and deadly party line in *Pravda* or the works of Marx or Lenin that are truly revolutionary today.

It must be admitted that the government of the Soviet Union has long known what rightist national security states are only now discovering: the gospel is dangerous. It must be destroyed, banned, discredited. If taken seriously, it can topple ideologies and governments. It can, quite simply, radically change the direction of lives and the very course of history. It can undermine the evil constructions of a malicious society and cause them to crumble. Like fire cast upon the earth, it burns away pretensions and injustice, lies and greed, lust and cruelty.

But there is a price to pay. Those who serve the "spoken Christ" will often suffer as he suffered. The Christ who comes to us in the freeing and hopeful words of the gospel is the same Jesus who died on the cross.

On March 24, 1980, Archbishop Oscar Romero of San Salvador did not celebrate the liturgy in the large, unfinished, and quite ugly cathedral in the center of the city. Instead, he began the Mass in the chapel of Divine Providence Hospital. He read the gospel of the day and then began his homily. As always, his words were simple and direct.

"We have just heard in the gospel that those who surrender

to the service of people through love of Christ will live like the grain of wheat that dies. This hope comforts us as Christians. We know that every effort to improve society, above all when society is so full of injustice and sin, is an effort that God blesses, wants and demands. We have the security of knowing that what we plant, if nourished with Christian hope, will never fail.

> This holy mass, this Eucharist, is clearly an act of faith. This body broken and blood shed for human beings encourages us to give our body and blood up to suffering and pain, as Christ did — not for self, but to bring justice and peace to our people. Let us be intimately united in faith and hope at this moment.[1]

At this point, Archbishop Romero was shot to death.

These last words of the murdered archbishop of San Salvador still echo, and the tragic loss of this noble Christian preacher is still mourned. There is no doubt in the minds of the poor people of his country that he is a martyr and a saint. His photo hangs in many homes. But why was he killed? Ambassador White, who was at the American embassy at the time, has said that he knows the murder was planned by a few of the richest and most important people in the country. They actually held a lottery to see who would take care of getting rid of him. A gunman was hired and the deed was soon done. But why did they do it?

The homily that Archbishop Romero preached on Passion Sunday, March 23, the day before he was murdered, rather clearly points to the "crime" for which he would pay with his life:

> Let no one be offended because we use the divine words read at our Mass to illuminate the social, political and economic situation of our people. Not to do so would be un-Christian. Christ desires to unite Himself with humanity, so the light He brings from God might become life for nations and individuals.
>
> I know that many are shocked by this preaching and accuse us of forsaking the Gospel for politics. I reject this accusation. I am trying to bring life to the message of the Second Vatican Council and the meetings at Medellín and

Puebla. These documents must be translated into the real struggle to preach the Gospel as it should be for our people.

Each week I go about the country collecting the cries of the people, their pain from so much violence. Each week I ask the Lord to give me the right words to console and to denounce. And even though I may be a voice crying in the desert, I know that the Church is making the effort to fulfill its mission....

Many statements from Christian groups expressed support for the letter we sent to the president of the United States. They support our desire that he not give military aid that contributes to the repression of our people. One of these statements, by the U.S. ambassador here in El Salvador, confirms from his experience that such aid from the U.S. always ends up being used for military repression.

I issue a special entreaty to the army, National Guard, police and military. "Do not kill; you kill fellow peasants, your brothers and sisters. No soldier is obliged to obey an order against the law of God."

The Church — defender of God's law, of the dignity of the human being — cannot keep quiet before such abhorrent actions. Reforms are useless if they leave the people so bloodied. In the name of God's suffering people whose cries rise up to heaven every day in greater tumult, I implore, I beg, I order, in the name of God Himself: "Cease the repression!"[2]

These words and those of his previous sermons had condemned him to death. It was somehow fitting that the archbishop should die while preaching, since it was in the service of the "spoken Christ" that he denounced "a situation of social sin," "a desire for power and domination, for discrimination of all sorts" (Puebla, paras. 28, 435).

Must martyrdom, either the dry martyrdom of scorn and calumny or the bloody kind represented by the body of Romero cut down in the midst of a liturgy, follow as the inevitable result of gospel proclamation? Perhaps it is not inevitable, but it has clearly become highly possible. As the Brazilian Leonardo Boff has said: "Martyrdom is possible because there are those who prefer to sacrifice their very lives rather than be unfaithful to their own convictions. The martyr has absolutes; situations can arise where his conscience requires acceptance of persecution and the sacrifice of his life in witness to the truth."[3]

But martyrdom is also possible because of those who bitterly reject the proclamation of freedom and the denunciation of slavery and evil which is the task of the Christian preacher. "There also exist mechanisms of domination and falsehood, implying the denial of God. In such circumstances, to proclaim God, truth and justice can only be done, without betrayal and sin, through persecution and death."[4]

The martyr-preacher never seeks his or her martyrdom. It is always imposed violently from outside. "It is not the punishment but the cause that makes true martyrs," said St. Augustine.[5] Oscar Romero and all the other martyr-preachers of every age defend the cause of Jesus and his brothers and sisters by dying. That cause is believed to be greater than life. While every preacher knows that it is not only necessary to speak the words of Jesus but also to imitate him, some begin to see that imitation of Christ involves a sharing in his insults and torture. "He was insulted and did not retaliate with insults; when he was tortured, he made no threats but put his trust in the righteous judge" (1 Pet. 2:23).

The "spoken Christ" present in our preaching teaches us how to be prophetic. But those who give him his voice today may also be led to the cross and his sacred passion. "You will be hated by all men on account of my name...you will be dragged before governors and kings for my sake...the disciple is not superior to his teacher..." (cf. Matt. 10:17–36). However, it is unhappily true that many persecuted preachers from South Africa to Lithuania and from Korea to Guatemala are not universally revered by their fellow Christians. In the higher circles of both the Protestant and Catholic churches there is a certain nervousness and deprecation when their names are mentioned. Yes, they would say, it is unfortunate that Duma, the seventeen-year-old son of the Methodist President, Dr. Simon Gqubule, is currently experiencing his second spell as a prisoner in solitary confinement in order to punish his father. And it is true that several Lutheran pastors were held in detention in Vendaland and claim to have been tortured. And there are, of course, the Anglican bishops deported from Namibia and South Africa.

But perhaps they became too involved in politics. Perhaps they forgot their true mission and became indiscreet.

And Fathers Betancourt and Cypher who were killed in Honduras; Maura Clarke, Ita Ford, Dorothy Kazel, and Jean Donovan who were murdered by the military in El Salvador; the twenty-eight-year-old pastor Hector Gallego who was "eliminated" in Panama; the young priests Juan Moran Samaniego and Rodolfo Aguilar Alvarez who were assassinated in Mexico — could it be that all of them and the dozens of others killed throughout Latin America allowed their teaching and preaching to become too political, too revolutionary? Could it be that the pastors who were jailed in Czechoslovakia and the Ukraine and the Philippines, and all of those who have been murdered in Argentina, Brazil, Guatemala, and Chile were somehow guilty of antagonizing the authorities by departing from the "spiritual" to preach a "political gospel"? Certainly there are those in Rome and Washington, Nashville and New York, London and Geneva who feel all of these preachers were ill-advised if not rash and reckless, and that they somehow brought their sufferings on themselves through a lack of diplomatic sophistication and curial *suavité*.

Jon Sobrino of El Salvador, however, speaks of the need for *political holiness*. As Archbishop Romero said, "A religion held with deep conviction leads to political involvement and tends to create conflicts in a country like ours where there is a crying need for social justice." A Christian holiness always presupposes that it is a response to God's will. Is it not his will "that the poverty and oppression of millions of human beings should stop, that there should be an end to their constant deprivation of human dignity, the horrible violation of their rights, the massacres, the mass expulsions, arrests, tortures and murders?"[6] The answer of a sincere Christian pastor will be a love which is a response to God's will that his people have life. It will be a reply to the present enormous suffering of the poor. It is what Sobrino calls "political love."

This type of love has characteristics that make it different from other forms of love.

In this first place it requires a *metanoia* to see the truth of the world as it is, in the manifestations of death, which are visible, and its structural causes, which are hidden and take care to be hidden, to see in this generalized death the largest fact and the most serious problem of humanity, the one which is the greatest challenge to the meaning of history and humanity, so that we do not imprison the truth of things through injustice (Rom. 1:18). It requires *pity* for the unhealed but not unhealable suffering of the oppressed majority, Jesus' pity for the multitude. It requires an awareness of *responsibility* when asked the question, "what have you done with your brother?" (Gen. 4:95) and co-responsibility for his condition and his destiny.[7]

This political love leads one to political holiness. It has its own ascesis which recalls fundamental Christian teachings. It involves *kenosis*,

going down into the world of poverty and the poor, a stripping of self; the ascesis necessary in order to denounce and unmask oppression, to have historical patience and solidarity with the poor. It favours the growth of a mature faith and hope in a situation where they will be tried to the utmost. It favours Christian creativity (pastoral, liturgical, theological, spiritual) generated from the underside of poverty.[8]

Before his own death, Archbishop Romero said about his murdered priests: "For me they are truly martyrs in the popular sense. They are men who went all the way in their preaching of solidarity with poverty. They are real men who went to the most dangerous limits to say what they wanted to tell someone, and they ended up being killed as Christ was killed."[9]

For political love leads to persecution. "This is the inexorable fulfillment of Jesus' preaching. Political love, unlike other forms of love, unleashes the specific suffering of persecution by all the powers of the world. Not all Christians, but political Christians are attacked, vilified, threatened, expelled, arrested, tortured and murdered."[10]

Is the political then to be avoided? Is it even possible for the preacher to avoid it? Although the pastor may rightly strive to avoid identification with parties and labels, as soon as a word is spoken about the urgent questions of life and death, war and peace, poverty and riches, nuclear arms and government spending, official priorities and real needs, then the sermon is already political. The blood of so many murdered preachers from the brutality of both the Communist and the "national security" forces reveals the political as a proper sphere for holiness. Indeed, Christian life for layperson and preacher today means involvement with politics. And much of our preaching must cut against governmental wisdom and popular illusions to plead for basic human social rights, to help bring about "bold and urgent" structural changes, as Paul VI said, and to denounce clearly the evils of selfishness and deception.

> God who is a holy mystery has come close to us: he has broken the symmetry of being either salvation or condemnation. And this nearness is doubly scandalous: it is a nearness of the mystery of God and a *special* nearness to the poor and oppressed. Because he loves them, God has come out on their side, fights against the idols of death and shows himself clearly as the God of justice who truly wants the life of the poor. And since Jesus, this is the new and scandalous holiness of God: coming close to the poor to save them and sharing their lot on the cross of Jesus.[11]

Is the preacher of today called to a "political holiness"? Is there any other way for a herald of the gospel who would tell the world that God truly loves the poor? Quite simply, is it possible for a preacher to avoid the cross? Archbishop Romero said, "It would be sad if in a country where murder is being committed so horribly we were not to find priests also among the victims. They are the testimony of a church incarnated in the problems of their people."[12]
Jon Sobrino insists:

> Political holiness is historically necessary today for the poor to receive the good news and for history to move toward the coming of God's kingdom. It is also important for the Church itself, so that with it, it may recover the truth of the Gospel and make this the foundation of its mission, and so that externally it may retain its credibility

which it can only keep among humankind today if it offers effective love for the poor.[13]

The otherworldly spirituality of the recent past had its dangers and temptations; now the preacher's political involvement will demand an alert intelligence, an acute sensitivity, and constant care. As Bishop Francisco Claver of the Philippines says:

If the Christian is to involve himself in politics, *he must do so as a Christian.* It sounds like the most sterile of formulas. And most simplistic. It probably is. But to Christians whose faith is put to the test daily by all kinds of outrages and inhumanities visited on the weak by the powerful for the sake of *their* power, it is heavy with meaning, very heavy. For it means we have to work mightily at all times for justice without ourselves becoming unjust. We have to strive to lessen the ills of poverty — to bring about economic development, yes — without ourselves turning materialistic and selfish. We have to struggle along with the powerless for their rightful empowering without ourselves becoming manipulative, power-mad, ruthless... because we seek to tell Caesar there are other things in life more important than, or at least as important as, physical well-being and comfort, power and domination, we come under persecution — by Christians.[14]

This is, of course, one of the great ironies of the contemporary martyrdom of Christian preachers. So much of the persecution comes from those who claimed "one Lord, one faith, one baptism." In Latin America especially, the first reaction to the blood of its martyrs was amazement and incredulity.

First, the martyrs were Catholics killed in countries which were culturally Catholic. They thus shattered the schemas according to which the Church undergoes martyrdom in the twentieth century only where atheistic Communism has seized power. Secondly, the martyrs were being killed in countries belonging to the apparently secular and tolerant western civilizations. This was a blow to the confident belief that fanaticism had collapsed in the West after the defeat of Nazi-Fascist irrationality. Finally, in the West, Christianity seemed to belong to the respectable order of values, and the churches to the core of powerful institutions. Latin America dislodged the habit of seeing the faith threatened solely by a marginal minority of radical intellectuals and young iconoclasts.[15]

A "cultural Christianity" has existed for many years side by side with what the Puebla documents called "a situation of social sin," "a desire for power and domination, for discrimination of all sorts" (Puebla, paras. 28, 435). Christianity had been vertical and disincarnate. Generations of preachers had offered a distant hope of heaven to the poor and sweet pieties for the reinforcement of the rich and powerful.

Moreover, since Latin American society is structurally linked with the enrichment and domination of the major western countries, the martyrdom of Catholics in Latin America has also become a denunciation of the hegemonic intransigence of the "North" and of the victims which post-industrial capitalism claims in Latin America, allegedly in the name of anti-Communism but in fact as part of the accumulation of wealth which it refuses to share (Puebla, para. 1209).[16]

As a group of Latin American Protestant pastors wrote in an open letter to North American Christians in September of 1978: "We Latin Americans are now discovering that quite apart from our own weaknesses and sins not a few of our miseries and frustrations rise up and are continued in a system which brings to your country substantial benefits, but which submerges us more and more in oppression, in powerlessness and death. In a word: your valued 'American way of life,' the opulence of your rich businessmen, your economic and military power is fed, in no little way, from the blood which flows from the open veins of Latin America."[17] The preachers who come to feel a responsibility to be "the voice of those without voice and of those who were silenced," who know that the poor must have the gospel preached to them and who denounce injustice and brutality soon discover that they are considered "subversive of the established order."

The six Jesuits murdered at the University of Central America were considered "leftist" because they spoke out for the poor. To ask for justice for those imprisoned and tortured, to work on behalf of the *campesinos*, to defend the oppressed means that one will be labeled a Marxist, an agitator, or even a terrorist. It becomes, therefore, a noble act to destroy such a danger to the nation. As the slogans painted on walls in El Salvador put it: "Be patriotic: Kill a Priest."[18]

Sometimes there have been attempts to create confusion and division among preachers of different Christian traditions. One day a group of young men were waiting in the parlor of Archbishop Romero in San Salvador. They wanted to talk with the archbishop. They said that they were Baptists from the "Primera Iglesia Emanuel" and that they had been invited to a meeting with the president of the republic. The government offered to give them money for their missions saying that the money that formerly was given to Catholics would now be given to them. The young Baptists said that they refused and had decided to work with the Catholic church by the side of the poor.

The blood of martyrs of all nationalities, Protestant and Catholic, mingles and becomes the seed of Christianity. Stanley Rother, a native of Okarche, Oklahoma, worked for thirteen years with the Cakchique people of Guatemala. He was a peaceful man who not only preached the gospel but worked to improve the health and the agriculture of his parishioners. But when the farmers of his parish were murdered by the army, he denounced the atrocities. He was murdered near his church in Santiago Atitlán the night of July 28, 1981.

In September of the same year, John David Troyer, twenty-eight years old, was shot and killed at his mission in the Department of Chalatenango, Guatemala, and his fellow missioner, Gary Miller, was seriously wounded.

Rother was a Catholic priest and Troyer was a Mennonite missionary; both dared to proclaim that the poor Indians of Guatemala are children of God and have dignity and rights. Both discovered that living the gospel and preaching it to others can lead to a persecution as real as any suffered by Laurence and Stephen, Cecilia and Agnes, Ignatius of Antioch and Polycarp. Catholic and Protestant, they joined the long list of Christian witnesses in a contemporary *Acta Martyrum* which rivals in numbers, courage, and heroic love the records of the early church. The blood of both of them poured out on the rich earth of Guatemala as their ultimate sermon.

The modern preacher-martyr knows what can happen. Dorothy Day and Daniel Berrigan were often in prison because of their eloquent use of symbolic action in the cause of Christian peace. But they were hardly surprised. Dietrich Bonhoeffer was probably the first clergyman to denounce on the radio the evil cult of the Führer and, from April 1933, to stand against the anti-Semitic laws. He was not a naive man. And Martin Luther King often spoke of the imminent possibility of violent death. In 1961 he said, "It may get me crucified. I may die. But I want it said even if I die in the struggle that 'He died to make me free.' "[19] During the Selma march in 1965, he told his followers: "I can't promise you that it won't get you beaten. I can't promise you that it won't get your home bombed. I can't promise you won't get scarred up a bit — but we must stand up for what is right. If you haven't discovered something that is worth dying for, you haven't found anything worth living for."[20]

King's sermons always contained the hope for freedom, and he always related it to his current struggles to attain freedom in this world. But when it seemed as if freedom was difficult to realize in this world, Martin King did not despair but moved its meaning to an eschatological realm as defined by the Black Church's claim that "the Lord will make a way somehow." The night before he was assassinated (April 3, 1968), King, in a Black Church worship service, restated that hope with the passion and certainty so typical of the Black preachers: "I don't know what will happen now. We have got difficult days ahead, but it doesn't matter with me, because I've been on the mountain top. Like anyone else, I would like to live a long life. But I'm not concerned with that. I just want to do God's will, and He has allowed me to go up to the mountain."[21]

Preaching involved walking a *via crucis* for Peter, Paul, and John, as we learn from the Acts of the Apostles. They preached, they were put in prison, they were whipped. But they had also been "on the mountain top" and yearned only "to do God's will." Once again, preaching is understood as a sharing in the cross of Christ, a coming down from the mountain with a vision and a mighty word but knowing that a crown of thorns, a scourge and cross may be waiting.

Maurice Barth describes the scene:

San Salvador, 1979, Sunday, eight in the morning, in the cathedral. People everywhere, mostly ordinary poor people. Suddenly, a wave of applause sweeps through the concrete nave. A short man comes forward in priestly vestments. He is about to celebrate mass and deliver a homily lasting over an hour, punctuated by applause. It will be a homily classical in style, but nevertheless "extraordinary," different from what the poor people have been hearing for centuries, trapped as they have been in a religion of submission and hope — hope for the next life. It will be different because it will be both the good news proclaimed *to* the poor and *their* word, arising out of the daily dialogues with a bishop who shares their day-to-day anxieties. It will be a homily which is a constant appeal to transcendence, considered not as an abstract notion or disembodied spirituality, but as an entry into a new world, a transfiguration of man, as individual and as a people, now.[22]

In the Soviet Union, Korea, the Philippines, South Africa, and Chile a biblical vision, a hope for justice, freedom, and peace rooted in God's promises and God's fidelity have been perceived as dangerously subversive!

Some catechists report from Guatemala:

Where they have found bibles, they have torn them up, trampled them underfoot or burned them. They say, "If you keep that up, next time we'll kill you. You have to give up the Bible." So people bury the bibles and the hymn books, but they continue to meet, not in houses but in the mountains, in secret. Our lives are of little importance. What matters is to do something for people, to make sure that our faith doesn't die.... The people know

that the blood of the catechists bears fruit.... The blood of
our friends is a light.... You ask why they are doing that
to Christians? It is because we have understood what the
Bible is.... We have begun to read the Bible and the words
we read are quite clear to us. We have the story of Moses,
who brought his people out of slavery, the story of Jesus,
who was persecuted from childhood. That is why persecution is severest against Christians, because they have
realized that for us the Bible is an awakening.... [23]

It has been an awakening not only for the poor farmers
of Central America but also for thousands of North American
pastors and people as they discover and are challenged by the
richness, the vitality, and the sharp edge of the biblical text. As
long as preachers used only "favorite texts" and conveniently
forgot to explore the "hard sayings," it was possible to comfort
but never challenge. But when the Lectionary is read each Sunday with a full interpretation of its thought and emotion and
when the least of Jesus' brothers and sisters begin to help us to
understand the Bible's explosive power, it is almost impossible
to return to the old secure paths.

It would be foolish to think that we risk or suffer as so many
Christians do in Latin America, Asia, or Africa. To show how
the way of Jesus judges our American racism, sexism, arrogant
nationalism, and greed may bring some harassment, but it can
seem trivial compared to death squads and torture.

Yet more and more American Christians are suspicious of
the "party line" of the great corporations and the military industry. More and more come to realize that anger can be a virtue
and that slogans and suppositions must be examined with great
suspicion.

The dangerous word of the Lord cuts into our lives, our society, and our church.

• 9 •

TO PREACH AS JESUS DID

Back in 1925 Gertrud von Le Fort expressed what countless numbers of our contemporaries deeply feel. In fact, how many of our parishioners might agree with her words after the Sunday sermon?

> Who shall deliver my soul from the words of men?
> From the distance they are clarion-calls, but drawing close
>   they turn to an idle tinkle.
> They advance with banners and pennants, but when the
>   wind rises, their brave show is scattered.
> Harken ye loud and presumptuous ones, wind-strewn chil-
>   dren of your own caprice:
> We are parched beside your well-springs, we are starved by
>   the meat you offer us, we have grown blind by the light
>   of your lamps.
> You are like a road that leads nowhither, like so many small
>   steps taken around yourselves.
> You are like a driving flood, the sound of your gushing is
>   forever in your mouth.
> You are the cradle of your own truth, tomorrow you shall
>   be its grave.
> Woe to you who would lay hold on us; only with God can
>   a soul be captured.
> Woe to you who would quench our thirst with beakers, a
>   soul must be slaked with eternity.
> Woe to those whom your vain heart teaches!

> A priest at the altar has no face, and the arms that raise
> the Lord are without dust or ornament.
> For when God bids us speak, He bids us be silent, and one
> who is kindled by His spirit is in darkness.[1]

All of us begin to feel that we are swimming in words. The dams of restraint and reticence are broken and the fields of our lives are flooded. Those who sense they will soon drown unplug the radio, sell the TV, and pull their Walkman earphones from their heads. But the noise keeps coming: the "ghetto blasters" on the bus, the bland "music to buy by" in stores and elevators, and now the loud but predictable tunes our telephones give us when we're put on "hold." We long for some "piped-in silence." Too much, far too much trite melody, cheap poetry, and weary, wooly, and weak prose. Some flee for a weekend or a lifetime to a cabin in the mountains. Others come to church, knowing of course that they will hear more words but hoping that they will be the important words, not the trendy, the cute, and the trivial.

The preacher looks out and sees Marie, whose husband died only a week ago. And then there is Peter, who has been out of work for a year. Not easy to get something when you're fifty-eight. Steve and Becky are there — their baby is due any day. But Sandy comes by herself now, since Ned left her and the children. Pat, who always sits in the last pew, knows how sick he is and has toyed with the idea of suicide. Agnes, in the front pew, is old and lonely. Flo and Andy are worried about their daughter in New York. And Andy Jr. is just worried about getting through high school! What will they hear today? Will they hear the Lord speaking? Will they hear a preacher who, like Jesus, has prepared for preaching in prayer and fasting, who has been to the desert, who has learned about suffering and joy, despair and hope? Can they also say about us:

> Now I know that the Lord speaks from you, because you
> have mastered His silence.
> You have learned it like a mighty speech, your words are
> only its heralds.[2]

To preach as Jesus preached. To speak words that will help open minds and hearts, so they may be flooded with living waters and not with the stagnant and muddy. Lives there a pastor who does not want to do it the Lord's way? Who does not look to the Lord who came preaching?

We tell stories, of course, because without parables and stories he did not teach them. We even try some visual aids, since we know he had a wonderful way of pointing at fig trees, flowers of the field, and birds of the air, of passing around a coin of tribute and placing a child on his knee. We try to stay close to his message, his themes, and his emphasis.

Yet something seems lacking. We know clearly that the times have changed, that the first century is not the same as the final years of the crazy twentieth, that Judea and Galilee have little in common with Ohio and California. We make adjustments. We know many people have never seen a live lamb outside of a zoo. We do what we can with mustard seeds in New York and with vineyards in Chicago. And a lot of time is spent explaining Samaritans to Texans!

We know Jesus was vivid, patient, and kindly. But we also realize he confronted his hearers and was polemical and disturbing. His preaching meant movement and risk; he left his roots and became itinerant. He went to anyone who would listen to him, in streets, markets, open fields, and private homes. He looked for an audience wherever people assemble, near a city gate or on the porch of the temple. He left his own family and district and became, as Michel Philibert observed, difficult to place professionally. Could he be called a rabbi, a healer, a prophet, an agitator, a wandering adventurer, a seeker of the most disreputable, the prostitutes and collaborators? He met the conflicting and changeable aspirations of his people, their longing for dignity and deliverance from disease and hunger and shame, their desire for glory and revenge. All would, in the end, be either disappointed or transformed by Jesus.

His words were urgent. The rich young man was offered his deliverance only once. "Behold, I set before you the way of life and the way of death" (Jer. 21:8). He will allow no delay. He does not suggest we "think about it and come back next Sunday." He demands an immediate decision. The teaching, the repetition, and the perseverance will come later.

The hearer is not allowed to discuss sin as an abstract concept. He or she is asked to break through a system of habits and shatter a way of living. Self-images must be pushed over and broken — now! The rich young man walked away, but many others stayed to hear more.

This first preaching announced God's kingdom and called for response, demanding a decision to break with the old circle, its attitudes and unholy customs. It led directly to the agony and joy of conversion.

Our Sunday sermons are not addressed to the crowds but to the "faithful" who, we piously hope, have already been converted. While conversion can be considered an ongoing process, a lifetime project, and while many of the "unconverted" drift into our churches for various motives, we know that most of us speak to congregations that, by and large, have come to know Christ and are trying with some success to follow his way. We are not itinerant. Traveling missionaries will always be needed to go into the streets with Jesus to search out and save what is lost. Indeed, no Christians, and certainly not the clergy, are completely excused from that primary responsibility. But that is not our Sunday morning task.

On Sunday morning we speak within the community. We address, for the most part, disciples. Constant "evangelization" is not helpful and can be, in fact, counterproductive. And yet, when we see Jesus preaching in the gospels, he is usually out on a hillside or in the crowded porch of the temple speaking to nonbelievers. He does not face a community of converts but rather crowds of men and women who hardly know his name. There are many gospel pages that can teach us his methods of basic evangelization, but where do we find the Lord preaching in a situation similar to ours? Is there any place where we find him giving a homily to disciples?

The homily that Jesus at least started to give in the synagogue at Nazareth certainly teaches us some important lessons about the nature of preaching, but his listeners could hardly be compared to ours. Although they had been his neighbors for many years, they proved to be anything but friends and disciples. They were quite ready to kill this preacher who dared to interpret the reading in such a radical way. "And when the people in the synagogue heard this, they were all very angry, and they got up and drove him out of the town and took him to the brow of the hill on which their town was built, intending to throw him down from it" (Luke 4:28–29). It is doubtful that any of the preacher-martyrs of later centuries had such an immediate and violent reaction to one short homily! We must look elsewhere to find Jesus preaching among disciples in a Christian community.

It is John, of course, who presents us with a wonderful picture of Jesus as preacher among those who had already accepted him. We know, however, that we are not to look in these chapters of John's Gospel for the *ipsissima verba Christi*, the very words of Christ himself, for surely this account of the farewell discourse was never meant to be a stenographic transcription! The author recreates in this last gospel a scene that occurred years earlier, and he fashions his chapters with theological purpose and poetic skill (but without the benefit of a tape recorder left under the supper table).

But this does not prevent us from coming to these pages with both reverence and curiosity. For this is the most complete account of what Jesus said to his apostles in that upper room on their last night together. Here, at this final and most poignant meal, Jesus used not only the signs of bread and wine, but also the signs that were his spoken words to express his love for his own. Preaching had an important place at this solemn supper as Jesus, with both memorable drama and touching simplicity, performed a community-forming liturgy and consecrated himself to his redeeming death. He then told his followers that they must do as he had done, in his memory.

We are allowed therefore to return to the Last Supper discourse in our search for words to continue our preaching. This "sermon" of Christ is not, of course, meant to be the unique homily, any more than the Our Father is meant to be the only Christian prayer. But, just as we study *Oedipus Rex* and *Hamlet* to learn the meaning of tragedy, we would do well to turn to these chapters of the Gospel according to John to discover something important about a homily.

Precise sequence and detail are certainly less important than the themes and mood of the Lord's farewell message. We are able to understand a good deal of the atmosphere and style of this "preaching" in that banquet setting. It may seem a bit bold to call the Last Supper discourse preaching at all, for John and Jesus probably would not have used such a label. Certainly most of today's preaching, in or out of a liturgical setting, has little in common with it. But that very fact might well be the heart of our problem.

If John's presentation of the final supper discourse seems somewhat disordered and repetitious, it is nonetheless vivid. In fact, the very disorder and repetition may be John's way of showing us the informal and conversational style of Jesus' communication. In the first lines of chapter 13 John tells us that Jesus "had always loved his own who were in the world, and now he was to show the full extent of his love." This refers to the coming passion and death of Christ in which he would show his love by laying down his life for his friends. But it also refers to what Christ would do and say in the upper room before his passion. He would show the full extent of his love by giving himself in the bread and the wine of the Eucharist, and by sharing his thoughts and feelings in his farewell discourse. Language, like the eucharistic gifts themselves, became a means of making love manifest.

The preaching of Christ on this occasion began with "silent language," the nonverbal language of dramatic action in the washing of his disciples' feet (13:3–5). The incongruity of Christ the Lord doing the work of a servant was a lesson of service and love, a dramatic image that the apostles could never erase from their memories. Christ, however, saw fit to underline the meaning of his action (13:13–17). An example was given — direct, simple, and taken from daily life — as were so many of the examples that Christ used as he preached. In this case, however, the example was fully acted out by Christ himself. It was an ordinary action for a servant or slave, but a most extraordinary one for a rabbi or teacher. Christ seems to have chosen it for its dramatic value in the context of the sacred Passover supper that was being celebrated. There can be little doubt that it captured the attention of the twelve and prepared them for what was to follow.

Christ also wanted his audience to learn something and then act upon that knowledge. "If you know this, happy are you if you act upon it." But we notice that this knowledge did not come through propositions and augmentations, but through a shared experience. Although Peter protested, all of the apostles actually had their feet washed by Christ. They lived through an event together, feeling that it was important and memorable but not knowing clearly what it all meant. Christ told Peter, "You do not understand now what I am doing, but one day you will" (13:6). In this dramatic prelude to his farewell discourse, Christ was depending more on intuition, the power of a common experience, and the surprise that would come from the example of such lowly service than on logic.

"After saying this, Jesus exclaimed in deep agitation of spirit, 'In truth, in very truth I tell you, one of you is going to betray me' " (13:21). The disciples looked at one another in bewilderment: whom could he be speaking of? Nervously they began to question Jesus. Once again, there was a good deal of nonverbal communication that the apostles picked up quite readily. Christ shared at least some small part of his emotional life with his disciples.

John recorded our Lord's empathy and his profound emotions, his kindness in drawing his disciples' attention to the religious and eschatological meaning of the coming events, rather than throwing them into panic by a simple announcement or by his anxieties when he considered his betrayal and imminent suffering. It is clear that Jesus convinced his listeners not with the power of the syllogism but with the depth of his involvement in life and in a poetic statement. The washing of the feet and the unmasking of the traitor were not bits of petty "playacting" but deeply moving experiences for Christ as well as the apostles. Lesser preachers may be concerned about "artistic distance" from their text and a scholarly detachment. We can find no indication of this "distancing" in the preaching of Christ as recorded by John.

This is not to say that Christ did not have control of his text. On the contrary, his control was excellent. Like a good poet, he chose his words for maximum effect. Like an experienced speaker, he touched his audience — in fact, he moved them so deeply that many years later they could still relive the scene. Even modern readers may find themselves filled with emotion in merely reading the discourse in translation, centuries after it was spoken. But this artistry of Christ followed Oriental traditions and not Western norms.

Since the Hellenistic influence, which had entered their country and found expression in Greek theaters, gymnasia, and statues, was abhorrent to all devout Jews, we should not expect to find Christ following classic models in speaking. A serene *via media* was never a Semitic ideal. When Christ walked by the Lake of Galilee, he carefully avoided Tiberius with its orderly Ionic columns in favor of the more Jewish Capernaum. Just as carefully did he avoid Hellenistic dialectical and systematically philosophical discourse in favor of the intuitive, the story, the poetic statement. Yet, if we agree that the maturity of a work of art is its inclusiveness, its awareness of complexity, its ironies and tensions, then we may grant that the Last Supper sermon is a work of art, but a work of art that is not only religious but strongly Semitic.

The various parts of the discourse are not in an orderly and logical sequence according to Western standards, and they have presented serious difficulties for readers trained to expect a precise development of topics. Instead, the style is "free-floating" and expansive. The talk moves in circles like an eagle over the Judean desert. The same topic is touched a number of times from a number of different points. There is always the chance of further illumination and deeper experience. The attention glides from one theme to another like the infinite variations of an Indian *raga*, but always there is a return and a repetition like a haunting refrain in Oriental music.

Certain literary characteristics can be recognized. Christ uses paradox with an artist's skill. There is the powerful paradox of the master washing the feet of his servants which, as we have seen, forms a striking prelude to his words. This is followed by the play of contrasts between the baseness of the traitor and the basic innocence and goodness of the disciples. Judas is unmasked by a prophetic gesture of Christ, and the evil of the man who had become like Satan is contrasted with the dignity and control of Jesus, just as the darkness of the night outside the supper room is contrasted by John with the Light of Israel who begins his hour of darkness. The faithful Lord is contrasted with the unfaithful Peter, and we sense another paradox when Jesus foretells that the chief of the apostles will deny his Lord three times before the cock crows.

As is frequently the case, Jesus uses figurative language to present a message. When he says: "... my way there is known to you" (14:4), Thomas immediately misunderstands. This provides Christ with the opportunity to explain and more thoroughly unfold his doctrine. It would almost seem to be a studied literary technique in which a metaphor or figurative language leads to misunderstanding, misunderstanding leads to dialogue, and dialogue leads to deeper exploration.

The allegory of the vine that Jesus presents at the beginning of chapter 15 is an echo of the beautiful song of the vine in Isaiah (5:1–7) and helps us to understand the Hebrew image. However, we are also reminded that a share in the Lord's sacrificial death and eternal life will come through the "fruit of the vine." While the sacramental reference is not direct, it is emphasized here just as the "bread of life" is emphasized as a pledge of life and union in chapter 6.

The metaphor of the vine would be rich in meaning for the apostles who, as Jews, would remember that the vine was an image of the chosen people (Jer. 2:21; Ezek. 15:2–8, 19:10–14; Hos. 10:1). Psalm 80 sets forth the history of Israel under the image of the vine. And, just before or shortly after Christ used the metaphor, these same apostles would have received the sacramental cup of wine from the hands of Jesus. There is, in Christ's metaphor, a profound meaning that gradually would unfold for the apostles and for the believing Christian community that would follow them.

The stylistic devices that may be discovered in the Last Supper homily should not lead us to think that Jesus spoke from a prepared text or that his artistry was not spontaneous. There is a sense of improvisation and an authentic informality. The farewell discourses are the spiritual testament of the Lord and a real farewell to the disciples whom he loved. Jesus spoke in the shadow of imminent death and with deep emotion. As we know, such an occasion can sometimes evoke the ideas, the rhythm, and the diction that may fashion a text of poetic greatness.

If the Western reader understands that in this homily several ideas are developed at the same time and that there are overlappings of themes that defy schematization, he or she will not feel a lasting frustration at the apparent disorder of the discourses. It is, perhaps, wiser simply to allow the important themes to rise to the surface and to study them not in some preconceived schema but at random. Without ever attempting, therefore, to exhaust the richness of Christ's preaching at the Last Supper, we may recognize in it the themes of *love, hope, peace, joy*, and *faith*.

A major theme of this preaching was announced when Christ gave his disciples a new commandment of love (13:34–35). But love, for Christ, was not an abstraction; he did not philosophize about it. Rather, he immediately pointed to an example of what he meant, an example that they had experienced. They were to love one another as he had already loved them, and this love would distinguish them as his followers. He led them to a community of love reminding them of the love and dedication that he had given them. His homily formed a bond of love and service, not through an appeal to ideal norms but through the memory of concrete experiences. The farewell discourse was without doubt a word of love.

Christ's eucharistic sermon was also a word of hope. As a good preacher, he responded to the mood that he felt in his audience. Peter and the others were concerned about him going away (13:36–37). Although Christ found it necessary to deflate the boasting Peter by telling him that he will have denied him three times before the cock crows, he understands his fears. He knew that these gruff fishermen, for all their tough appearances, were in need of encouragement and hope (14:1–2).

The homily established a community founded on hope in God and in Jesus Christ. Certainly, Christ preached no naive "art of positive thinking" — in fact, he would soon tell his disciples of the pain and agonies that await those who dare to follow such a master and to question the *status quo*. But neither would he allow them a spirit of despondency and despair (14:18–20). Their unity with Christ was the source of their hope and brought the promise of apostolic success.

To illustrate this, Christ turned once again to an image that his hearers could easily grasp: "I am the vine and you the branches. He who dwells in me, as I dwell in him, bears much fruit; for apart from me you can do nothing" (15:5). Jesus seemed to identify himself with his words; he dwells in the Christian (15:7). This suggests that the force of Christ's words is deep and penetrating, reaching not only the mind but the whole person. Their action may be subliminal, working on the unconscious as well as the conscious. Nor is their effect transitory, for they "dwell" with the Christian and make prayers efficacious. They bring confidence just as they unite us with Christ, the true vine. They cut away the barren branches and make the fruitful branches more fruitful still. "You have already been cleansed by the word that I spoke to you" (15:3).

This Passover sermon that Christ spoke to his disciples was not only a word of love and hope but also a word of peace. It was, however, a special kind of peace, the peace of Jesus Christ and not some kind of worldly tranquillity (14:27). His peace was to be an inner peace that had no necessary connection with secular disorders, with war or the peace of the diplomats. It was a parting gift that was offered through the words of the Savior. Language served as the instrument of a mysterious but real peace that would set troubled hearts at rest.

The preaching of Christ in the setting of the eucharistic meal, even though the crucifixion was only hours away, was also a pledge of joy (16:22). Christ had sympathy for the apostles' present sorrow. He knew of still greater anguish to come, and he clearly predicted that his disciples would share in his suffering (15:18–21). But though the warning was a grim one, Christ made no effort to soften the hard facts of persecution, insisting that their suffering would not be forever (16:20–22). Though the preaching of Christ made them aware of harsh realities, it was not meant to increase their sadness. On the contrary: "I have spoken thus to you, so that my joy may be in you, and your joy complete" (15:11).

The words of Christ in this prototype of homiletic, eucharistic preaching were not words of recrimination. They did not wound or excoriate; they did not berate or scold. This is not to say that Christ never spoke in such a way, but rather that in the context of this first eucharistic liturgy Christ chose to heal and encourage. His words had for their expressed purpose the bringing of his joy, which would make the joy of his disciples complete.

But again, it was clear that the joy which Jesus wanted his followers to have was something far deeper than a superficial gladness. Indeed, he recognized that his necessary warning of future martyrdom had brought consternation and fear (16:2–4). He did not tell them at first because they were not ready. Here in this atmosphere of comradeship, in the atmosphere of the ritual Passover supper when the suffering and salvation of their ancestors were solemnly remembered, they could be told what would be too hard to hear on another occasion (16:7). The Lord wanted them to know that he does only what is for their ultimate good. He felt a bond of love that united him with this little group of frightened fishermen, whose foibles and foolishness he knew so well.

The apostles themselves must have been very much aware of their failings, their infidelities, their bickering, and their cowardice, which would be most evident in just a few hours when only John, the youngest of them all, would dare to follow Jesus to Calvary. What must have been the force of hearing the master whom they had served so imperfectly calling them his friends — friends for whom he would lay down his life (15:12–15)? It was another example of the feeling that Christ had for his listeners. It was more than respect for them. It was more than a considerate acknowledgment of their dignity and worth. It went beyond kindness. It was far more than the affection of a master for his servants. It was, as Jesus himself said, the love of friendship in which, without self-interest, the good of others is willed. It brought to them a mysterious but real inner peace and joy.

The preaching of Christ at the Last Supper was also a word of faith. Jesus revealed something of his mystery. His homily explained more about himself and his Father. It both asked for faith and strengthened faith.

Christ was telling his disciples that he was going to his Father's house to prepare a place for them. Thomas was confused and asked, "Lord, we do not know where you are going, so how can we know the way?" Christ's reply to this question was, in fact, a request for still greater faith and trust in him: "I am the way; I am the truth and I am life; no one comes to the Father except by me" (14:3–6). He did not tell them he would show them the way, that he would teach them the truth, or that he would help them to find life. Instead, he claimed to be the way and truth and life! It was truly a remarkable claim, and one that had to be received in faith or rejected in disbelief.

Christ identified himself with his Father and then asked for the faith of the apostles in his words (14:7–9). He did not attempt to "prove" the mystery but only asked for a loving trust and confidence in the truth of his word. His word was the word of the Father himself (14:10–12).

The faith that Christ required in his followers was not a cold intellectual assent to a list of revealed truths but a warm and living commitment, a habitual and loving trust in the words and in the person of the Messiah. It was a faith that must not be separated from good works, from obedience and love (14:21).

But Christ knew that in the human heart faith would sometimes suffer serious assaults, and so his preaching word was meant to strengthen faith and renew their tired hearts (16:1). By the end of chapter 16, the disciples at least claimed to understand at last and to respond with faith (16:29–30). Jesus replied to their profession of faith with a question that sounds ironic: "Do you now believe?" Perhaps he felt they had spoken a little too glibly. But he soon continued with words of great kindness and hope (16:33).

The farewell discourse ends with the beautiful prayer that occupies all of chapter 17. Jesus looked up to heaven and spoke directly to his Father, praying for his disciples in words full of unity and love (17:20–21). Just as Christ has been sent into this world by his Father, so these disciples have been sent forth into the world by Christ so that others might put their faith in him "through their words." The preaching of love, hope, peace, joy, and faith must continue.

All during this Last Supper preaching, the apostles felt free to question Jesus. There was no constraint, no reluctance to enter into a dialogue with him. Simon Peter, John, Thomas, Philip, Judas — "the other Judas, not Iscariot" — all these are mentioned by name as having asked questions. The disciples not only made comments and asked questions but even entered into some discussion among themselves (16:17). Although this was a ritual supper and the most solemn feast of Passover, the atmosphere in the upper room was quite informal and, once Judas Iscariot had left, both cordial and intimate. Christ was "among his own." He knew their weak natures (16:31), yet they were his followers and his friends. His words would be continued by their voices. And during this Last Supper together he needed their companionship and simple loyalty and wanted to share with them his thoughts and final testament.

The respect and reverence, which the disciples clearly had for Jesus, and the majesty of that moment which they seemed to sense, did not silence them. Christ was their "master" and now their "friend" — they did not fear him as a "boss" or "tyrant." Although Christ's emotions changed and moved powerfully through the farewell discourses, at no time did he personally frighten these men. At times his words were difficult, mysterious, even stern. At times there seems to have been a touch of irony. And certainly they were words of great seriousness and majesty. But at no time did Christ speak without a deep compassion and human tenderness. The apostles did not, of course, fully understand what Christ said and did on that solemn night, but they did share in his feelings and experience what he wanted them to experience. They did have a conversation with him, an exchange of words, ideas, and emotions that would have a lasting effect.

Such, then, was the preaching of Jesus Christ at that first Eucharist. Such were its themes and emphasis, its style and moods, its setting and atmosphere. It gave an example of dialogue and participation. It offered vivid and memorable illustrations and shared experiences. The homily that Christ spoke bound his disciples to one another, to him, and to his heavenly Father (17:22–23). The words of Christ prepared for and continued the effect of the Holy Eucharist; they were words that established communion — among his disciples and between them and their God. And, just before the apostles left the upper room, the preaching of Christ led to prayer. Jesus spoke to the Father and, as Matthew and Mark indicated, they all sang the Passover hymn before going out to the Mount of Olives.

Today, the words and actions of Christ are repeated. We clergy in this century do what Christ commanded should be done: we take the bread and wine, as Christ did, and offer them as food and drink to the people, using the very words of Christ — "This is my body; this is my blood." But, unfortunately, the preaching which should continue that of the Last Supper often has little resemblance to the farewell discourses of Christ.

Christ spoke, first of all, to companions around that supper table whom he knew and understood. The author was careful to note not only what Christ said to the impetuous Peter but how he answered Philip and Thomas. It was a highly individualized discourse, an exchange among comrades who had shared three years of hardship and happiness together, and not a "set speech" to be repeated at other times. But the quality and tone of this preaching, the themes that were developed, the purpose for which Christ spoke, the simplicity and energy of his style, the warmth and intimacy of the setting — surely all these things should guide the preacher who would speak today.

There in the cenacle in a most wonderful way the Lord linked sacrament and word.

· 10 ·

THE PERSON WHO PREACHES

It is easy to say that a new poetry and prophecy are needed for Christian communication. But how can it happen?

The times are strange; the hucksters are noisy; the skies are gray with sadness. The "good news" seems to be shouted down by the tragic bad news of war, starvation, child abuse, terrorism, pollution, and general hardness of heart. When the problems of international greed, massive injustice, lust for power, and corruption of the innocent are so intimidating, can the voice of the "spoken Christ" in the preaching of his very limited brothers and sisters be heard at all?

Can the humble Christian, aware of the commission received at baptism and confirmation to tell others about Jesus, but who has no television show, no comfortable budget, and no special "show biz" charism, still say the words that will help destroy the satanic darkness which anyone who reads the newspapers or catches a news broadcast knows is there? Can our simple words about Jesus effect change, precipitate and accelerate the process of conversion from sin, both personal and institutional, and truly free people from the cold torrents that inundate their hopes and poison their lives? Isn't it too much to expect from any words? What poet, playwright, or novelist would dare to think that his or her most brilliant lines might achieve such results?

But it happens! The Lord is master of his word. It is alive

and active. It cuts more deeply than the two-edged sword. Yet do we honestly believe it?

We who are called to proclaim the gospel — by church authorities, by ordination, by God-given talents, or merely by circumstances — seem timid and almost voiceless. When we do speak it is mezza voce and with great hesitancy. Are we afraid of the gospel's explosive power and revolutionary impact? Are we excited about our own vocation to speak it with faith, power, and joy? Are we enthusiastic about the fact that, unlike so many, we really have something great to say in our lives? Not the clever words of a glib salesperson, a talented lawyer, or a witty entertainer. Not the inane and even deceptive words that are spoken and written in such astounding numbers. But the welcome words that can save the despondent from despair. The burning words that cast fire upon the earth to burn away the tangled undergrowth of viciousness and greed. The daring words of forgiveness and justice and love.

The Christian people want preachers who will "follow a straight course in preaching the truth" (2 Tim. 2:15). For "every prophet who teaches the truth without putting it into practice is a false prophet" (*Didache*). Therefore holiness of life is necessary. A strong formation in Christian spirituality is of the greatest importance. The preacher must pray.

But "grace builds on nature" as an old and wise saying puts it.

If this is so, then a good preacher must first of all be a good person. We should find in him or her those attractive human qualities we would look for in any good human being, especially in one who will be a "public person" appearing before many people as an important speaker. Does he or she have those qualities of mind and heart that we would even hope to find in a good politician or television announcer? Is he or she intelligent and alert to what is happening in the world and in human lives today, compassionate and caring, especially for the poor and marginalized, hungering for justice and freedom for all? Is he or she excited about what is true, good, and beautiful, showing a healthy Christian anger concerning the false, evil, and ugly? Does this man or woman prepare, as Karl Barth suggested, with the Bible in one hand and the daily newspaper in the other?

Is the preacher sensitive and unafraid of honest emotion, not coldly intellectual and yet not ruled by emotions nor anti-intellectual. He or she should value reason highly and should be able to think as a philosopher even as he or she respects and treasures the intuitions of the poet.

Perhaps the greatest human quality that preachers will need (since they will be speaking fifty or more times each year to people who are often jaded and weary of talk) is creativity. Imagination, so often ignored in American education, must be valued by the preacher. Fresh relationships between scripture and daily life must be constantly discovered. Words and images, stories and metaphors — these must be precious for preachers as they must be for anyone who would move people through language. They must be artists with words. But their poetry must be the poetry of the people, avoiding both the obscure and the sentimental. They can learn from Royko and Joyce and Hemingway, from short stories and essays and *Time* magazine.

But all of these human qualities are not enough in Christian preachers. They feel themselves called — and their calling has been tested and approved by the church — and now they stand before the congregation as prophets who not only speak about God but also speak for God!

Those who would dare to speak for God and with the voice of Christ must be more than just good people with a full complement of human virtues. They must be more than just competent oral communicators with a "gift for words" and clear orderly minds. They must be in close union with God.

They will not, of course, be "confirmed in grace," sinless and angelic. But they must be persons of faith. With a loving trust in Jesus Christ and his mercy, they will try to follow the gospel way which they present to their audience. Even though they themselves are judged by the very words that they speak, they are not afraid to present the challenge of the gospel which they discover in the Bible texts and in the noble traditions of the church. In prayer and reading they try to listen to the Lord and present to the people the words that Jesus would have them hear today.

But still more is needed. Preachers must know the gospel that they dare to proclaim, but they must also know the "world" in which they preach that gospel. They must know the needs and cares, the pain and joy of the people so that they may speak to minds and hearts, moving them to conversion, deeper Christian prayer, or action. Therefore the disciplines of anthropology, sociology, psychology, and politics take on an obvious importance. Whatever will help the speaker understand those who receive the message cannot be ignored. The history, literature, and art of a people can lead to a great sensitivity to their hopes and spiritual hunger. "Pop" culture (TV, songs, movies, commercials) have something to teach anyone who would speak effectively to young people today.

But it is still not enough. "The one who speaks is to deliver God's message" (1 Pet. 4:11). The message is delivered in vain, however, if the listeners do not really "hear," do not draw meaning from the message. Therefore the art of rhetoric is not to be despised.

As we watch our restrictive and sectarian theology wither and die in the winds that originated in the Second Vatican Council, we also hear the death gasp of an exhausted "rhetoric of religion." We feel ourselves in a time of great crisis and radical, though not clearly understood, transformation. If classical rhetoric does not adequately serve the gospel today, we wonder where we will find a rhetoric that will serve.

Without denying the importance of persuasion in the preaching of evangelization and of exposition in the preaching of catechesis, the sermon is now frequently understood as "homily," i.e., a familiar conversation about the "wonderful things of God" in the intimate setting of the sacramental meal. It may be conceived not as an "oration" on a sacred theme but as the oral interpretation of a text that is an integral part of the liturgy.

This is, frankly, a new orientation. It requires experimentation and risk, new approaches and new techniques, and — more importantly — it also asks for a change in attitude. The preacher is no longer to see himself as a sort of pious Demosthenes in a pulpit, as an aggressive solo performer attacking enemies of the holy faith, or even as a thundering prophet, with the sword of logic in one hand and the club of emotion in the other, setting out to defend morality or doctrine. A new self-image is called for, at once noble and self-effacing. The preacher is now asked to be an oral interpreter of the word of God rather than an orator, a poet with a fresh language rather than an intellectual with speculative ideas, and an artist with sensitivity and imagination rather than a metaphysician trained in abstraction. For many pastors such a shift is patently impossible. They would find such a radical change of emphasis incredible and absurd.

Although the rhetorical rules of the ancient Greeks and Romans may no longer be adequate for effective preaching, this does not mean that rhetoric is not found in the new and developing patterns of Christian oral communication. In the new preaching, as in poetry, language may be used to move men and women to action, and therefore it may be rhetorical. But it is a language of friendship that encourages us, in freedom, to follow Christ in a community of faith and love.

The Book of Daniel (9:23) calls Daniel a *vir desideriorum*, a man of strong and holy desires. Although the preacher must beware of exploiting his audience through the crass manipulation and the coercive strategies of the commercial and political persuaders, he is, after all, a man who desires the kingdom of God and has heard the call to speak out concerning it. Even though he has the obligation to hand on the message of Jesus Christ as it has been handed down to him, he must, at the same time, be something of a prophet, a *vir desideriorum*, who uses a speech of affection and not of neuter propositions. What Josef Jungmann has said of prayer may also be said of religious speech: "The best kind of prayer and contemplation is that which stirs up holy desires in the prayerful heart and fills it with the love of God and admiration for his greatness."[1] But while the man of prayer may feel that he should not restrict the soul in its activity and disturb its peace by seeking for precise words and well-turned phrases, the prophet or preacher would share his desires with others and therefore becomes a poet speaking of his vision and a rhetor welcoming others to enter into it.

To do this, however, the preacher finds it necessary to go beyond semantically purified speech, what Richard Weaver calls "a simple instrumentality, showing no affection for the object of its symbolizing and incapable of inducing bias in the hearer."[2] He must find a language, verbal and nonverbal, that will attract, excite curiosity and interest, and reveal the Christian life as beautiful and good.

Jungmann remarks:

In community prayer, however, external forms are absolutely essential, for it is only by means of external forms that a community act can exist at all. We are not pure spirits. Every corporate and social activity among men must therefore have its visible, perceptible focus in time and place, otherwise we cannot make contact with one another. And when our corporate act is directed towards a social work which is spiritual in character, as is the case with prayer and worship, then *symbols* have to be found, in word and gesture, so as to give adequate expression to this spiritual element and make it a truly corporate expression.[3]

In this wider sense, therefore, the problem of the preacher is poetic, since he must also find symbols to give expression to the "spiritual element," and at the same time rhetorical, since he would make the preaching event a truly corporate expression and experience. If, following the example of Jesus at the Last Supper, we practice a preaching that draws us into a communion with God and our neighbors, we must reject the compulsion of forensic oratory and encourage the subtle persuasiveness of the good poet who invites us to share in his experience. In this task, Aristotle's *Poetics* may be of more help than his *Rhetoric*.

At any rate, for the preaching that would lead us to prayer, Greek oratorical and philosophical models have little to offer. Argumentation and discursive discourse may also have their own eloquence, but they do not greatly help us to come close to the Christian mystery, to the constantly renewed *admirabile commercium* spoken of in the liturgy of the Christmas season. Rudolf Bohren becomes quite rhetorical himself when he says:

If preaching as God's Word is an event, then our preaching must avoid the hellenistic Greek concept of the word like the plague. It must not concern itself with general truths. Where points are brought up for consideration, where preaching soars to the heights of a philosophical lecture, there the angel of the plague stalks through the churches and slays the congregation. That is the abomination of desolation in the sanctuary of preaching, the fact that Greek thought largely dominates the pulpit — if, indeed, any thought goes on at all. If suppressed yawns fill

so many of our Evangelical churches the way clouds of
incense fill Catholic churches, it is because the form of
preaching has largely been determined in hellenistic Greek
fashion by content rather than by the event. The pastors
have been through the humanistic education of the Gym-
nasium, and therefore enter upon their preaching office
equipped with the worst presuppositions imaginable, having been schooled in Greek thought. It was not by chance
that Jesus drew his messengers not from the academies but
from fishing boats and tax offices.[4]

The rigidly geometrical and fairly simple Greek patterns in
thought and rhetoric are being replaced by a preaching that is
both more complex and more freely formed.

It is essential that preachers gain and maintain the attention
of their hearers. Even if they speak loudly and clearly, avoid
distracting mannerisms, and show some animation in their expression and gestures, they may easily lose their audience if their
message seems tedious and bland. Can it be that the unpardonable sin is to bore people with the word of God?

The preacher works with words as a craftsman might work
with wood or metal. He or she must present a message in words
that will be faithful to the truth and also hold the interest of
old and young. The preacher should have a "feel" for words, for
their power and their beauty and be both prophet and poet.

The preacher is, of course, involved in weekly and often daily
oral communication. It may be unfair to compare his or her
Sunday sermon to the highly gifted and trained speakers on the
stage and in television and radio, but such comparisons are inevitable. Preachers should, at least, not be an embarrassment.
Therefore they must have basic skills of public address, know
how to write and speak clearly and vividly, how to maintain
attention and to persuade.

It is the task of the homiletics faculty to try to bring these
qualities and skills together. It is, clearly, not easy. Homiletics professors must be generalists, enthusiastic about the many
facets of religion and communication. They must read widely
and share their knowledge of both the gospel and the world.
They must respect each seminarian, trying to help each discover
his or her gifts and mission as a preacher.

While we might find inadequate the classic definition of preaching as "truth through personality," it is certainly true that God works in different ways in different people. It is an impossible task therefore to describe the "ideal" preacher.

Although preaching has a history from which we can learn very much, it is done today in a context far different from that of Paul or Chrysostom, Bernard or Luther, or even Fulton Sheen. Whether it be evangelical or catechetical preaching, or a homily done in the setting of the sacraments, it is addressed to audiences, sophisticated or unlettered, who are influenced by science and technology, free-swinging capitalism and the noisy voices of Madison Avenue. Audience analysis becomes a high priority.

The purpose of preaching can no longer be seen as individual conversion and growth in piety. Christian preaching must lead to the transformation of society from the ways of selfishness, violence, and greed to the paths of justice, peace, and purity. It will only be the brave preacher who will challenge the assumptions of our indulgent society, since both preacher and congregation have been deeply influenced by its propaganda and its charm.

Preaching, as Augustine points out in *De Doctrina Christiana*, part 4, is about "speaking the truth": "He who seeks to teach in speech what is good... that is, to teach, to delight, and to persuade, should pray and strive that he be heard intelligently, willingly and obediently." To learn, to be moved, to be changed in attitudes and action, to be led deeper into the heart of the gospel, accepting the attitudes of Jesus Christ toward life and its problems, toward the realities of a world moving rapidly into the next millennium, to be helped, encouraged, inspired, allowed to taste and see the goodness of the Lord — all this the Christian people hope for from their preachers.

In some sense everyone on a seminary faculty teaches preaching. No subject in the curriculum can be isolated from the pulpit. While the sermon is not to be fashioned in the style of a classroom lecture or an article in a theological journal, it is nourished by all that goes on in a good seminary course. Especially when the professor does not forget that the students are destined for pulpits and altars and not for libraries and universities!

And since preaching, like every art, is primarily learned through imitation, the example given by preachers in seminary liturgies is indeed powerful. Every daily homily has a positive or negative effect. In fact, every preacher whom a student hears in a parish, a university chapel, or even on TV says something good or bad about this ministry. Possible role models, both positive and negative, are everywhere.

But we must be realistic about today's students. They hardly remember a world before inflation, AIDS, the sexual revolution, cable TV, computers, and Ronald Reagan. They are older; they come from more diverse backgrounds and often with little previous Christian training. Like many of their generation, they avoided the liberal arts in favor of science and other "practical subjects." Many have had no previous experience in public speaking and very little work in written composition. Many are still victims of "stage fright."

There are frequent self-doubts — but also doubts about the church and its doctrine and discipline. In addition, some seminarians have been wounded by personal and family problems, latent anger and uncertainty. They are, in a word, men and women of their generation with its strengths and weaknesses.

Quite naturally, all these factors have an effect in the pulpit. The priest or minister of tomorrow will be, perhaps more obviously than in the past, not only a "wounded healer" but also a "wounded preacher." They will be expected to be articulate, to have wit, imagination, and a life formed by the gospel. They may also have a good deal of questioning and pain.

They will need encouragement and support for serious study and preaching. They must have courage to say not only what is consoling but also what is challenging and frequently not to the taste of some of the people in the pews (who are no longer so docile and not at all hesitant to let the new minister or priest know their views!). They will need zeal and fortitude in order not to be discouraged or overwhelmed by the task. They should have both confidence in God and in their own talents, but also a healthy humility. And certainly a sense of humor will help!

Clearly help for the preacher must come from many sources outside of the formal homiletics class. But it is in that class that many questions surface and answers can be sought, and it is there that the importance of preaching can be explicitly stated and appreciated.

Yet the pastor who is already in the pulpit also must continue to think and talk about preaching. It is both burden and delight, task and mystery. It deserves, like the church itself, both a critical questioning and a loving contemplation.

We preachers and lectors are entrusted with the word of God. We are commissioned to proclaim it to the whole world in season and out of season. There are certainly few things we might do that are more noble, more beautiful, or more satisfying. We are servants of the "spoken Christ" and, as Paul said, "coworkers with God." It is right that we appreciate our dignity and the value of our calling. It is proper that we strive to be holy as our message itself is holy.

How then must preachers behave, what must they do in their own lives, how can they be willing cooperators so that Jesus may really speak through them? For, after all, they are not cold and lifeless tools. They have freedom. They may refuse their cooperation. They remain personal, free beings with individual strengths and weaknesses, talents and idiosyncrasies.

If they would dare to speak the word of God, they must first listen to the word of God. Lambert Claussen says:

> The office of preachers has two facets, one directed toward God and one toward men. The one is receptive and the other productive. Scripture expresses this in the two words *Ro'e* and *Nabi*, meaning prophet. *Ro'e* signifies "the seer," "the beholder," "the contemplator." God often spoke to the prophets in images and visions. *Ro'e* is the same as "hearer of the word." *Nabi* means "the speaker," "the announcer of the Word." When a Word of the Lord came to them, it was always the divine erupting into their lives. Thus they spoke of the hand of the Lord touching, overpowering, and weighing down upon them. They spoke of the Spirit of the Lord overshadowing, descending, seizing, laying hold of and pouring itself into them. It was their duty to open themselves to this divine eruption and not to flee the Lord as Jonas attempted.[5]

Both the pastor, the ordinary minister of the word for some time to come, and the layperson, who will be called to preach more and more, must let the gospel penetrate deeply and form their mode of life. The true prophet can speak only the word that has first been nourishment for him. In the Old Testament

Ezechiel vividly described his own calling to this mysterious
and mighty office:

> "You, son of man, listen to the words I say; do not be a
> rebel like that rebellious set. Open your mouth and eat
> what I am about to give you." I looked. A hand was there,
> stretching out to me and holding a scroll. He unrolled it
> in front of me; it was written on back and front; on it was
> written lamentations, wailing, moanings. He said, "Son of
> man, eat what is given to you; eat this scroll, then go and
> speak to the House of Israel." I opened my mouth; he gave
> me the scroll to eat and said, "Son of man, feed and be
> satisfied by the scroll I am giving." I ate it, and it tasted
> sweet as honey (2:8–3:3).

As Gustaf Wingren has said:

> The really great preachers... are, in fact, only the servants
> of the Scriptures. When they have spoken for a time the
> very words of the passage, the quotations from the Bible,
> come to have such power as if the Word sounded forth
> for the first time. It gleams within the passage itself and is
> listened to: the voice makes itself heard. The passage was
> perhaps read at an earlier point, but it was not heard be-
> cause of multifarious thoughts in the mind of the listener
> which got in its way. The preacher has since been at work
> on these obstructing thoughts, that is, he has been con-
> tending against the power of the enemy, and now at last
> the passage is heard, at last the Word (*verbum*) has broken
> down argumentation (*ratio*).[6]

Preachers use many texts. Some of these may be written and
some unwritten. Some may be of their own composition, but
frequently they work directly with a text written by another.
The most important of these, however, will always be the text
of the sacred scriptures that they must try to present in all of
its literary and religious richness. They must be more, therefore,
than exegetes. They must be holy.

They are called to the highest realm that is possible in oral interpretation for either Christian or Jew. They are called to interpret the word of God himself. Karl Rahner has said:

> To the poet is entrusted the word. He is a man who can utter the great words pregnantly (*verdichtet*). Every man speaks great words — as long as he has not sunk into a spiritual death. Everyone calls things by their names and in so doing, continues the work of Adam his father. But the poet has the vocation and the gift of saying such words pregnantly. He may say them in such a way that through his words, the things — as though set free — enter into the light of others who hear the word of the poet.... He [God] can come in no way other than as the word — without taking us already away from the world to Himself. For He should give Himself to us precisely in that which He simply as the Creator of realities outside Himself cannot reveal. This is possible only because there is something — one thing only — in the world which belongs to God's own reality: that reference redeemed from muteness, that reference which points beyond all created things — the word.[7]

The preacher is to be, therefore, the instrument of God's coming to us. It is, of course, one thing to attempt to bring the full intellectual and emotional content of a secular work of art to an audience. It is something far more mysterious to function as a means of salvation, to speak words that bring not only an esthetic experience but the possibility of eternal life. The preacher can only cry out with Jeremiah:

> Ah, Lord Yahweh: look, I do not know how to speak: I am a child!
>
> > But Yahweh replied,
> > "Do not say, 'I am a child.'
> > Go now to those to whom I send you
> > and say whatever I command you.
> > Do not be afraid of them,
> > for I am with you to protect you —
> > it is Yahweh who speaks!"

Then Yahweh put out his hand and
touched my mouth and said to me:
"There! I am putting my words into your mouth.
Look, today I am setting you
over nations and over kingdoms,
to tear up and to knock down,
to destroy and to overthrow
to build and to plant" (1:6–10).

Preachers soon know that they have been sent not only to
build and plant, but also to tear up, knock down, destroy, and
overthrow. Their words heal and delight the heart, but because
they are the words of God they can also cut and burn, over-
throwing the vanities of men and bringing judgment both on
the listeners and on those who dare to pronounce them.

Indeed, the words of Christ tear into the smug and inhuman
leaders, the arrogance of official religion, and the hypocrisy of
the self-righteous. These words, not surprisingly, earned Christ
crucifixion at the age of thirty-three. Preachers may find themselves wondering what they will earn them.

They can, of course, soften their harshness and conceal their
rugged annoying shape — but then they know that such interpretation has an empty sound. They have betrayed their text;
they have, really, dishonored their audience.

Christ had greater respect for his listeners; he was willing to
risk something for them. They were important for him.

That is why, to jolt them out of the placid mentality in
which man has listened to sermons since the world began,
Christ reminds them of their own experience, of the cruelty
of this world, of the law's delays, of the blatant triumph of
moral wrong. To make his own special devastating point,
he will go to any lengths. He is quite prepared to compare
his own beloved Father to a lazy judge who will at least be-
stir himself to shake off an importunate widow. *Anything* to
get the spark going across the gap that separates God from
the real in the mind of man, an insulation so effective that
man is not even conscious of it, and yet it becomes terribly
evident in the complacency of religious people when with

astounding naïveté they think to pass God's judgment on the prostitute.[8]

The thick hard crust of familiarity that has come to surround the words of Jesus must be broken so that the life that is there can be experienced. The love and power of Christ must be felt through the words that have been entrusted to the preachers.

In the word alone there lives and is known the transcendence which frees from death. The word alone can make God, as the God of the mysteries, so present for the man who does not yet see God, that this presence not only *is* in grace but indeed is *here* for us. The word as the primordial sacrament of transcendence is thus capable of becoming the primordial sacrament of known presence in the world of the God who is above the world.[9]

To speak this word, to speak of faith and love when the preacher is empty of faith and love, is a sin far greater than any lie of an artist or failure of a poet. The preacher feels, and rightly so, that one may easily be a noisy bit of sounding brass, a mere tinkling bell whose selfishness and lack of charity, whose dreary litany of sins make a mockery of the spoken words. One must of necessity talk of Christ, think of Christ, move in his presence. But in doing so, one is compelled to say with Peter, "Depart from me for I am a sinful man, O Lord!" Isaiah well understood the tension and the anguish of someone called to preach:

> What a wretched state I am in! I am lost,
> for I am a man of unclean lips
> and I live among a people of unclean lips,
> and my eyes have looked at the King,
>   Yahweh Sabaoth.

Then one of the seraphs flew to him, holding in his hand a live coal that he had taken from the altar with a pair of tongs. With this he touched Isaiah's mouth and said:

> See now, this has touched your lips,
> your sin is taken away,
> your iniquity is purged.

Then he heard the voice of the Lord saying: "Whom shall I send? Who will be our messenger?" He answered, "Here I am, send me" (6:5–8).

From the preaching of Christ and his apostles until the end of the world the word of God is dependent on the words and voices of men and women. In the Christian religion there must always be those who — though aware of their unclean lips, clouded minds, and errant hearts — will welcome Isaiah's seraph with the burning coal and will say, "Here I am, send me."

Far from being exempt from human suffering and failures, those who preach should experience an anguish that is especially acute. It is their splendor and agony to look toward both God and their fellows and to speak of the perfect Father in the language of his imperfect children. This challenge is not the least of Christianity's mysteries.

> Silence is the sacrament of the world to come;
> words are the instrument of this present age.
>
> —St. Isaac the Syrian
> (Letter no. 3)

NOTES

Preface

1. Caesarius of Arles, *S. Caesarii Arelat. Sermones,* ed. G. Morin (Maredsous, 1937), vol. 1. serm. LXXVIII, 2, pp. 309–10 (translation mine).

2 • Talking about Jesus

1. Clodovis Boff, "Emerging Third World Church," *World Parish: Maryknoll's World Apostolate Bulletin* 26, no. 234 (April 1986).
2. See Willard F. Jabusch, *The Person in the Pulpit* (Nashville: Abingdon Press, 1981), p. 27.

3 • Rising Expectations

1. Terence Eagleton, *The New Left Church* (Baltimore: Helicon, 1966), p. 118.
2. Ibid., p. 119

4 • The Necessary Word

1. Gerhard Ebeling, *God and Word* (Philadelphia: Fortress Press, 1967), pp. 3–5.
2. *La Documentation Catholique,* no. 1338, col. 1261 (October 16, 1960).
3. Michael Schmaus, *Preaching as a Saving Encounter* (Staten Island: Alba House, 1966), p. 65.
4. Ibid., p. 69.
5. Ibid., p. 76.
6. Willard F. Jabusch, *The Kingdom of God* (Chicago: ACTA-Musica Pacis, 1987), no. 8.

5 • The Rise and Fall of the Pulpit

1. Domenico Grasso, *Proclaiming God's Message* (Notre Dame, Ind.: University of Notre Dame Press, 1965), pp. 225–26.
2. Ibid., p. 223.
3. *Living Worship*, April 1967 (Washington D.C.: Liturgical Conference).
4. Ibid.
5. Grasso, *Proclaiming God's Message*, p. 224.
6. Yngve Briloth, *A Brief History of Preaching* (Philadelphia: Fortress Press, 1965), p. 87.
7. Ibid., p. 87.
8. Ibid., p. 94.
9. Ibid., p. 144.
10. Jerome, "Commentarium in Ecclesia," in *Sancti Eusebii Hieronymi Opera Omnia, Patrologiae Latinae*, ed. J.P. Migne (Paris, 1866), tomus XXIII, 1039A (translation mine).
11. Bernard of Clairvaux, "In Festo Omnium Sanctorum Sermo i, 3," in *Patrologiae Latinae*, ed. J.P. Migne (Paris, 1866), tomus CLXXXIII, 454 (translation mine).
12. *Didache* 11:10 in *La Didache: Instruction des Apôtres*, ed. J.-P. Audet (Paris: J. Gabalda, 1958), pp. 447–51 (translation mine).
13. Lucien Deiss, *God's Word and God's People* (Collegeville, Minn.: Liturgical Press, 1976), p. 306.

6 • Savoring the Text

1. Marshall McLuhan, *The Gutenberg Galaxy* (Toronto: University of Toronto Press, 1965), p. 1.
2. *A Gerard Manley Hopkins Reader*, ed. John Pick (New York: Oxford University Press, 1953), p. xxii.
3. Jean Leclercq, *The Love of Learning and the Desire for God* (New York: Fordham University Press, 1961), p. 18.
4. Ibid., p. 90.
5. Louis Bouyer, *Introduction to Spirituality* (New York: Desclee Company, 1961), pp. 52–53.
6. Ibid., p. 53.
7. Ibid., p. 54.
8. Ibid., p. 57.
9. Ibid., p. 72.
10. Celestin Charlier, *The Christian Approach to the Bible* (Westminster, Md.: Newman Press, 1958), p. 134.
11. Ibid., p. 135.

12. Ibid., p. 136.

13. Ibid., p. 137.

14. Henri Daniel-Rops, *What Is the Bible?* (New York: Hawthorn Books, 1958), pp. 14–15.

15. Charlier, *The Christian Approach to the Bible*, p. 139.

16. Ibid., p. 141.

17. Charles Moeller, "Is it Possible, in the 20th Century, to be a Man of the Bible?" in *The Liturgy and the Word of God*, Papers given at the Third National Congress of the Centre de Pastorale Liturgique, Strasbourg, France, 1958 (Collegeville, Minn.: Liturgical Press, 1959), p. 129.

18. Ibid., p. 130.

19. Hans Urs von Balthasar, "God Has Spoken in Human Language," in *The Liturgy and the Word of God*, pp. 35–37.

20. Moeller, "Is it Possible . . . to be a Man of the Bible?" p. 156.

21. St. Justin Martyr, *The First Apology*, chap. 67, 3–4; *P.G.* 6, 428; in *Writings of St. Justin Martyr*, trans. Thomas B. Falls (New York: Christian Heritage, 1948), pp. 106–7.

22. Augustine Cardinal Bea, "The Pastoral Value of the Word of God in the Sacred Liturgy," in the *Assisi Papers*, Proceedings of the International Congress of Pastoral Liturgy (Collegeville, Minn.: Liturgical Press, 1957), p. 83.

7 • A Touch of the Poet

1. Marshall McLuhan, *Understanding Media* (New York: McGraw-Hill, 1967), p. 71.

2. Ibid., p. 70.

3. Kurt Kranz, *Art: The Revealing Experience* (New York: Shorewood Publishers, 1964), p. 133.

4. Ibid.

5. McLuhan, *Understanding Media*, p. 36.

6. Ibid., p. 39.

7. Stuart Hall and Paddy Whannel, *The Popular Arts* (Boston: Pantheon Books, 1967), p. 58.

8. McLuhan, *Understanding Media*, p. 61.

9. Ibid., pp. 310–11.

10. Ibid., p. 215.

11. Frederick Buechner, *A Room Called Remember* (New York: Harper and Row, 1984), p. 151.

8 • The Explosive Word

1. See Oscar Romero, *A Martyr's Message of Hope* (Kansas City, Mo.: Celebration Books, 1983), as quoted in *Maryknoll* 78, no. 3 (March 1984): 42.

2. Ibid., pp. 39–42.

3. Leonardo Boff, "Martyrdom: An Attempt at Systematic Reflection," in *Martyrdom Today*, ed. Johannes Baptist Metz and Edward Schillebeeckx, *Concilium*, no. 163 (New York: Seabury Press, 1983), p. 12.

4. Ibid.

5. S. Augustini Episcopi Enarratio, "In Psalmum XXXIV, Sermo 2, 13," in *Patrologiae Latinae*, ed. J. P. Migne (Paris, 1845), tomus 36, col. 340 (translation mine).

6. Jon Sobrino, "Political Holiness: A Profile," in *Martyrdom Today*, p. 19.

7. Ibid.

8. Ibid., p. 20.

9. See Jon Sobrino, *Resurrección de la verdadera Iglesia* (Santander, 1981), pp. 177–209, 243–66; "Persecución a la Iglesia en Centroamérica," *Estudios Centroamericanos* ECA 393 (San Salvador: 1981), pp. 645–64.

10. Sobrino, "Political Holiness: A Profile," p. 20.

11. Ibid.

12. Ibid., pp. 22–23.

13. Quoted from *Cry of the Church*, ed. Jose Marins, Teolide Trevisan and Carolee Chanona (Quezon City, Philippines: Claretian Publications, 1983), p. 36.

14. Francisco Claver, "Persecution of Christians by Christians and the Unity of the Church," in *Martyrdom Today*, pp. 27–28.

15. Juan Hernández Pico, "Martyrdom Today in Latin America: Stumbling-Block, Folly and Power of God," in *Martyrdom Today*, p. 37.

16. Ibid., pp. 37–38.

17. P. Ferrari M. P. y Equipo, *El Martirio en América Latina* (Mexico City: Misiones Culturales, 1982), p. 11.

18. See Martin Lange and Reinhold Iblacker, *Witnesses of Hope* (Maryknoll, N.Y.: Orbis Books, 1981), p. 107.

19. Quoted by James Cone, "Martin Luther King: The Source for His Courage to Face Death," in *Martyrdom Today*, p. 76.

20. Ibid., p. 76.

21. Ibid., p. 78–79.

22. Maurice Barth, "Basic Communities Facing Martyrdom: Testimonials from the Churches of Central America," in *Martyrdom Today*, p. 43.

23. Translated from the French text in DIAL (Diffusion Amerique Latine, Paris), no. 107. This testimony is from women catechists.

9 • To Preach as Jesus Did

1. Gertrud von Le Fort, *Hymns to the Church* (New York: Sheed and Ward, 1953), p. 19.
2. Ibid., p. 28.

10 • The Person Who Preaches

1. Josef Jungmann, *The Liturgy of the Word* (London: Burns and Oates, 1966), p. 7.
2. Richard Weaver, *The Ethics of Rhetoric* (Chicago: H. Regnery, 1953), p. 7.
3. Jungmann, *The Liturgy of the Word*, p. 7.
4. Rudolf Bohren, *Preaching and Community* (Richmond: John Knox Press, 1965), pp. 63–64.
5. Lambert Claussen, "The Mystery of Preaching," *The Word: Readings in Theology* (New York: 1964), pp. 193–94.
6. Gustaf Wingren, *The Living Word: A Theological Study of Preaching and the Church* (Philadelphia: Fortress Press, 1960), p. 202.
7. Karl Rahner, "Priest and Poet," in *The Word: Readings in Theology* (New York: P. J. Kenedy, 1964), pp. 9–12.
8. Sebastian Moore, *God Is a New Language* (Westminster, Md.: Newman Press, 1967), p. 75.
9. Rahner, "Priest and Poet," p. 12.